A Training Guide for College Tutors and Peer Educators

A Training Guide for College Tutors and Peer Educators

SALLY A. LIPSKY
Indiana University of Pennsylvania

Boston Columbus Indianapolis New York San Francisco Upper Saddle River
Amsterdam Cape Town Dubai London Madrid Milan Munich Paris Montreal Toronto
Delhi Mexico City Sao Paulo Sydney Hong Kong Seoul Singapore Taipei Tokyo

ASC
LB
2331
.L57
2011
C.6

Executive Editor: Sande Johnson
Editorial Assistant: Clara Ciminelli
Vice President, Director of Marketing: Quinn Perkson
Executive Marketing Manager: Amy Judd
Production Editor: Annette Joseph
Editorial Production Service: Elm Street Publishing Services
Manufacturing Buyer: Megan Cochran
Electronic Composition: Integra Software Services Pvt. Ltd.
Interior Design: Elm Street Publishing Services
Cover Designer: Linda Knowles

For related titles and support materials, visit our online catalog at www.pearsonhighered.com.

Library of Congress Cataloging-in-Publication Data
Lipsky, Sally A.
  A training guide for college tutors and peer educators / Sally A. Lipsky.
    p. cm.
  Includes index.
  ISBN 0-13-714508-X
1. College teaching.   2. Tutors and tutoring.   I. Title.
  LB2331.L57 2011
  378.1'25—dc22

                                                           2009034578

Printed in the United States of America

10 9 8 7 6 5 4 3 2 RRD-VA 14 13 12 11

www.pearsonhighered.com

ISBN-10: 0-13-714508-X
ISBN-13: 978-013-714508-9

To my family, with love
and gratitude

Sally Lipsky's academic background and work experiences have centered on public education—from elementary to the postsecondary levels. Upon graduation from the University of New Mexico (B.S. elementary education), she began her career as a Title I reading instructor with the Houston (TX) public school district. After earning an M.Ed. in reading education from Texas Southern University, she taught in the Pittsburgh (PA) public schools. She earned a Ph.D. in language communications and adult education from the University of Pittsburgh and continued her career at Indiana University of Pennsylvania, where she has worked for over twenty years as a faculty member in the Developmental Studies Department, College of Education and Educational Technology. Her work involves coordinating academic support services and peer assistance programming; supervising paraprofessional peer educators; teaching first-year seminar courses and a peer educator training course; and developing promotional, evaluation, and outcomes assessment procedures. She has made numerous professional presentations and written about aspects of postsecondary learning, including the text *College Study: The Essential Ingredients* (in its second edition) published by Pearson Education. Furthermore, as a member of the College Reading and Learning Association (CRLA), she has chaired the Learning & Study Skills Special Interest Group. As a member of the National Association for Developmental Education (NADE), she has chaired the Peer Assistance Programs Special Professional Interest Network. To this day, she remains fascinated with the process of learning and committed to the value of public education.

BRIEF CONTENTS

CONTENTS

CHAPTER 3 Incorporating Critical Thinking and Questioning Skills   32

CHAPTER 4   Assessing Students' Learning   44

CHAPTER 5   Collaborative Learning and Group Work   55

CHAPTER 6 Tutoring as a Proactive Process   68

PREFACE

*The most important aspect of successful
tutoring is tutor training.*

— Hunter Boylan
National Center for
Developmental Education

A Training Guide for College Tutors and Peer Educators provides a comprehensive, multidisciplinary, and relevant training experience for readers. The intended audience for this text is tutors, peer educators, academic mentors, and similar academic support leaders at the postsecondary level. The text covers research-based components of successful peer assistance and can be used to train tutors for one-on-one sessions as well as leaders for group- and course-based sessions.

Beginning with Chapter 1, "The Power of Peers: Your Role as a Peer Educator," each chapter covers a topic important to the readers' roles as facilitators of students' learning. Content focuses on how tutors and peer educators convey subject-related information as they guide students toward success with college-level course work. By means of engaging activities, try-it-out experiences, and self-reflection, readers gain valuable knowledge and practice for their tutorial roles. As they progress through chapters, readers rehearse and evaluate peer-helping techniques, the same techniques that they will apply in their jobs as tutors and peer educators.

Features

CONCEPTUAL FRAMEWORK

Each chapter establishes a framework for content based on theoretical models of learning. Readers gain knowledge of underlying reasons for recommended peer-helping practices and, as a result, are more likely to follow through with implementing these practices in their work with students.

CHAPTER ORGANIZATION

Content of chapters mirrors appropriate methods for presenting material in an academic support session:

- *Opening activities* to introduce the content and focus students' attention
- *Activities within chapters* to assess students' understanding of each subtopic
- *Closing activities* to sum up content and check for understanding and learning

As they complete chapter content, readers experience the organization and procedures that bring about effective peer-led sessions.

Application exercises. Readers are exposed to a variety of thought-provoking and relevant examples and try-it-out activities. Included are structured observations, problem-solving scenarios, case studies, and role-playing of recommended techniques.

Integration of learning strategies. Interspersed within chapters are a range of strategies that promote active learning. Starting with an analysis of their own cognitive learning styles (visual, auditory, and tactile/kinesthetic modalities, and personality type), readers practice learning strategies and familiarize themselves with ways to introduce these strategies into their academic support sessions.

Self-monitoring exercises. Readers analyze aspects of their learning and study systems, including the process of setting and assessing personal goals. By monitoring their own progress, tutors and peer educators are better equipped to share this process with students. Readers are held accountable for their development as peer educators—the same process of self-regulation and responsibility that they will be conveying to students.

Suggestions from experienced peer educators. At the ends of most chapters are comments and recommended techniques from experienced tutors and peer educators. Reading about others' suggestions helps to guide and motivate the novice peer educator.

Lastly, to complete chapter activities effectively and master the content, readers are expected to put in time, effort, and thought—the same ingredients that a college student should use when learning new and important subject matter. Keep in mind that well-trained tutors and peer educators approach their jobs as prepared, skillful, and confident leaders. Ultimately, effective training of tutors and peer educators strengthens the overall quality and success of an academic support program.

For the Instructor

DELIVERY SYSTEM

As a flexible means to provide uniform training of tutors and peer educators, the text can be adopted for a credit-bearing course, as well as a series of noncredit workshops or seminars. Furthermore, the text can be used in various learning settings: instructor-led, self-paced, or distance education. The Instructor's Manual includes sample lesson plans for the instructor, as well as chapter instructions for students. The chapter instructions can be copied or placed online for students in self-paced or distance-education arrangements.

PROGRAM CERTIFICATION INFORMATION

Text chapters incorporate topics needed for certification from the College Reading Learning Association (CRLA) and National Association for Developmental Education (NADE). The Instructor's Manual contains information and materials, including sample assessment tools and templates, to use when applying for certification for Tutoring Programs (CRLA) and Course-Based Learning Assistance (NADE).

SUPPLEMENTS

- **Instructor's Manual (ISBN 0137145063)**

The Instructor's Manual that accompanies the text contains:

- Answer keys
- Lesson plans
- Supplemental exercises, examples, and role-playing scenarios
- Chapter instructions for individual readers in a self-paced setting
- Program certification information
- Sample course syllabus and topic outline that are blueprints for a credit-bearing course

- **Student Workshop Training PowerPoint Slides (download only) (ISBN 0137145543)**

    To access the Instructor's Manual and PowerPoint for this text, go to the Instructor's Resource Center, available to instructors exclusively through the Pearson IRC: www.pearsonhighered.com/pearsonhigheredus/educator/profile/ ircHomeTab.page

ACKNOWLEDGMENTS

I thank the following people for their professional comments, critiques, and suggestions regarding the text: Kathleen Buttermore, Walsh University; Ronald Weisberger, Ed. D., Bristol Community College; Sherry Wynn Perdue, Oakland University. In addition, I thank my colleagues at Indiana University of Pennsylvania—Carmy Carranza, Susan Dawkins, Arden Hamer, and Paul Hrabovsky—for their expert advice and support. Furthermore, I am grateful to Sande Johnson, executive editor at Pearson Education, for her astute guidance and perseverance with this project. Finally, I thank the cadre of paraprofessional peer educators, whom I have worked with and learned from over the years. I value their numerous ideas, their collaboration in the workplace, and their devotion to excellence. With deep appreciation, I acknowledge their many contributions to this text.

PEARSON mystudentsuccesslab™

Succeed in college and beyond!
Connect, practice, and personalize with MyStudentSuccessLab.

www.mystudentsuccesslab.com

MyStudentSuccessLab is an online solution designed to help students acquire the skills they need to succeed. They will have access to peer-led video presentations and develop core skills through interactive exercises and projects that provide academic, life, and career skills that will transfer to ANY course.

It can accompany any Student Success text, or be sold as a stand-alone course offering. Often students try to learn material without applying the information. To become a successful learner, they must consistently apply techniques to their daily activities.

MyStudentSuccessLab provides students with opportunities to become successful learners:

Connect:
· Engage with real students through video interviews on key issues.

Practice:
· Three skill-building exercises per topic provide interactive experience and practice.

Personalize:
· Apply what is learned to your life.
· Create a personal project that will be graded and can be posted to your portfolio.
· Journal online and set short- and long-term goals.

JAMES
freshman

MyStudentSuccessLab provides tools and support for students and instructors:

Student Tools/Support – Supplies these tools in addition to the video, exercises, and projects:
   Resources – Use of Plagiarism Guide, Dictionary, Calculators, and a Multimedia index of Interactive case studies and activities.
   Assessments - Includes Career Assessment tool, Learning Styles, and Personality Styles.

Instructor Tools/Support – Saves class prep time and supports implementation while engaging students:
   Sample syllabus – Ensures easy course implementation.
   Instructor's guide – Describes each activity, the skills each addresses, an estimated student time on task for each exercise, and a grading rubric for the final Apply activity.
   Additional Assignments – Suggests extra activities to use with each topic:
   · General activity related to an important objective for each topic.
   · Internet Assignment (e.g. Google "You Tube" video on topic) to find a video on key strategies and write a critique and present it to the class.
   · Resources usage – ie. Read and take online notes on the main points of the Understanding Plagiarism guide.

MyStudentSuccessLab is easy to use and assign. Visit **www.mystudentsuccesslab.com** for additional information. Technical support at http://247pearsoned.custhelp.com.

CUSTOMIZE THIS BOOK WITH

PEARSON LEARNING SOLUTIONS

FOR STUDENT SUCCESS AND CAREER DEVELOPMENT

The Pearson Custom Library Catalog

With Pearson Custom Library, you can create a custom book by selecting content from our course-specific collections. The collections consist of chapters from Pearson titles like this one, and carefully selected, copyright cleared, third-party content, and pedagogy. The finished product is a print-on-demand custom book that students can purchase in the same way they purchase other course materials.

Custom Media

Pearson Learning Solutions works with you to create a customized technology solution specific to your course requirements and needs. We specialize in a number of best practices including custom websites and portals, animation and simulations, and content conversions and customizations.

Custom Publications

We can develop your original material and create a textbook that meets your course goals. Pearson Learning Solutions works with you on your original manuscript to help refine and strengthen it, ensuring that it meets and exceeds market standards. Pearson Learning Solutions will work with you to select already published content and sequence it to follow your course goals.

Online Education

Pearson Learning Solutions offers customizable online course content for your distance learning classes, hybrid courses, or to enhance the learning experience of your traditional in-classroom students. Courses include a fully developed syllabus, media-rich lecture presentations, audio lectures, a wide variety of assessments, discussion board questions, and a strong instructor resource package.

In the end, the finished product reflects your insight into what your students need to succeed, and puts it into practice. Visit us on the web to learn more at www.pearsoncustom.com/studentsuccess 800-777-6872

CHAPTER 1

The Power of Peers

Your Role as a Peer Educator

OPENING: FOCUS QUESTIONS

Before reading the chapter, answer the following questions. Your answers will help you to focus your attention on key topics and to predict main ideas within the chapter. After completing the chapter, you will be asked to provide clear, thorough, and descriptive answers to these questions.

1. What is a peer educator?
2. What is the role of a peer educator?
3. What personal benefits can I expect from working as a peer educator?
4. How can I manage my time more effectively?
5. What are the key elements of a successful personal goal?

The student's peer group is the single most potent source of influence on growth and development during the undergraduate years.

— Alexander Astin, researcher and author

What Is a Peer Educator?

For the purpose of this text, peer educators are defined as tutors, Supplemental Instruction leaders, academic mentors, and similar student leaders who provide academic support and enhancement at the postsecondary level. Peer educators tend to work in student learning or academic assistance centers, tutoring or writing centers, developmental studies departments, or other educational support programs in two-year or four-year colleges and universities. Typically, peer educators are undergraduate students, though at some institutions graduate students, staff members, or professional tutors lead academic assistance sessions.

Peer educators lead tutorial sessions, either one-on-one or in small groups, or in course-based sessions. Course-based sessions refer to regular discussion/homework/review sessions for students enrolled in targeted sections of courses. Models of course-based assistance include Supplemental Instruction, Peer-Led Team Learning, Peer-Assisted Study Sessions, Structured Learning Assistance, Peer Assistance Learning, and comparable programs. At many institutions, peer educators provide a major, and sometimes the only, component of academic assistance for the undergraduate student body.

Role of a Peer Educator

As you probably recall, the academic expectations of students at the postsecondary level differ greatly from the expectations of students still in high school. In elementary through high school, adults (teachers and administrators) are responsible for the education of children (students). On the other hand, at the postsecondary level, students are considered to be independent adults responsible for their education. As adults, students register for their courses and decide whether to go to class and whether to complete schoolwork. Additionally, students in college receive their final grades as well as the bill for their education.

This transition from education as a "child" to education as an "adult" can be daunting for students, especially for traditionally aged students who move directly from high school to college. A major role of the peer educator is to guide students from dependent, "childlike" learning that they were accustomed to in high school toward more independent, "adultlike" learning that is expected of them in college.

The term *pedagogy* refers to instruction of students as "children"; the term *andragogy* refers to instruction centering on students as "adults." Malcolm Knowles (1980) summarized key differences between pedagogical and andragogical learning. These differences form a basis for describing a peer educator's role, which is to guide the college student from learning as a child (pedagogy) toward learning as an adult (andragogy). Figure 1.1 summarizes key differences between pedagogical and andragogical approaches toward instruction.

FIGURE 1.1 Pedagogy versus andragogy

	Pedagogy: *learning as a child*	Andragogy: *learning as an adult*	Examples for peer educators
Self-concept	Students are dependent on instructors to manage learning.	Students are independent and self-directed. Instructors guide students toward assuming responsibility for their learning.	*Students bring at least one question to each session.*
Experience	Students have narrow ranges of experiences. Students receive information from the experienced instructors.	Students have wider ranges of academic and personal experiences, which are valuable resources in a learning setting.	*Students supply examples that explain a concept.*
Readiness for learning	Instructors employ standard, step-by-step curricula based on students' developmental readiness according to age and grade.	Students' social and career interests determine content. Instructors include relevant, real-life activities, as well as social interaction.	*Pairs of students work together on an activity.*
Orientation toward learning	Students acquire knowledge for future use. Instruction is organized according to subject and difficulty levels.	Students expect learning to be for current use. Instruction includes problem-centered content and higher-level thinking.	*Leader presents a complicated, multi-step problem that students solve.*
Motivation to learn	Students are motivated by external rewards and punishments.	Students are motivated by curiosity and internal incentives to improve and master the content.	*At the end of a session, students identify what they learned and what they need to improve on.*

ACTIVITY 1.1

ANDRAGOGY AND PEER ASSISTANCE

A goal of peer assistance at the postsecondary level is to develop independent, responsible, lifelong learners. To maximize the success of students with whom they work, peer educators should incorporate the five components of

Continued

ACTIVITY 1.1 *Continued*

andragogy, or adult learning, as listed in Figure 1.1, under the column Andragogy: *learning as an adult*.

1. Read the examples listed in the far right column. Then, add other examples of how peer educators can incorporate each of the five components.

2. Explain each example to another peer educator. Have either of you observed this strategy?

FACILITATOR OF LEARNING

A major responsibility of peer educators is to assist students with *how to learn* college-level content. Skillful peer educators employ techniques that show students how to understand and remember difficult subject matter. As such, peer educators guide or facilitate students' learning.

Bear in mind that peer educators do *not* present themselves as experts on the subject matter or as substitute teachers or professors. In the peer educator role, it is quite acceptable to be unsure of an answer or to tell students, "I don't know." However, as a facilitator of learning, it is crucial that you guide students regarding how to solve the problem or how to find the needed information.

PEER EDUCATOR'S ROLE AND DEVELOPMENT OF STUDENTS

Your responsibility to guide students toward more independent, "adultlike" learning refers to all students, regardless of age. Though older, nontraditional students tend to be more physically and emotionally mature and more focused on career choices, they still approach college-level academics with many of the same needs as do traditional 18- to 22-year-old students (Chickering & Reisser, 1993).

Arthur Chickering (1993) created a universal model describing the psychosocial development of college students. This model consists of seven vectors, each highlighting an area of affective, social, intellectual, or personal development (see Figure 1.2, left-hand column). As a framework explaining college students' evolving behaviors and attitudes, Chickering's model is useful in your peer educator role. Note that the seven vectors do overlap and are not linear in nature. Students progress through the vectors with varying speeds, directions, and amounts.

In Figure 1.2, the right-hand column contains examples of how you, the peer educator, can boost the development, competence, and confidence of students in your academic support sessions. Each of these items is clarified within the chapters of this book. As a concluding activity in Chapter 9, you will be directed back to Figure 1.2 with the purpose of adding other examples.

FIGURE 1.2 Student development and peer educators

Students' psychosocial development Chickering's vectors (1993)	Examples of peer educators' role
1. Developing intellectual, physical, and interpersonal competence	• Actively involve each student in your sessions. • Call on students by name, and wait for them to answer questions. • You are viewed as a "model student"; therefore, pass on recommended learning and study behaviors to students. • Provide regular feedback to students to increase their sense of competence and confidence with course work.
2. Managing emotions	• Provide plenty of reassurance for both novice and returning students. • Incorporate anxiety-reducing techniques in your sessions. • Encourage students to develop a supportive network of family and friends. • Refer students who seem overly anxious, angry, or depressed to the campus counseling center.
3. Moving through autonomy toward interdependence	• Suggest that students organize their own study group for difficult courses. • Let students know that you expect them to complete homework and attempt problems before attending your session. • In your sessions, have students figure out answers to questions and problems. Provide opportunities for students to assist others. • Show students how to monitor their own learning and performance in courses.
4. Developing mature interpersonal relationships	• For group and course-based sessions, periodically direct students to sit beside and introduce themselves to a person they don't know. • Incorporate collaborative activities; periodically mix up groupings so that students are working with different people. (Females more than males tend to welcome collaborative activities.) • Create a welcoming and comfortable setting in your sessions. • Do not tolerate sexist, racist, or other bigoted comments in your sessions.
5. Establishing self-identity	• Showcase those behaviors and attitudes that are related to success. • Encourage students to assess personal weaknesses and areas of improvement, and then encourage them to seek advice about how to improve. • Encourage students to provide personal examples when explaining concepts.

Continued

FIGURE 1.2 *Continued*

6. Developing purpose	• Work with students on setting personal goals. • Relate subject matter to individual career goals. • Refer students who are undecided about a major or career to the campus career services office.
7. Developing integrity	• Incorporate activities requiring higher-level thinking and reasoning skills, such as defending points of view or providing evidence supporting an opinion. • Call attention to the personal satisfaction that comes with mastering a subject and understanding content thoroughly. • Have students review their individual and collective accomplishments. • Direct students to evaluate the working group's productivity and members' contributions.

Benefits for You, the Peer Educator

Most peer educators regard their positions as more than just another campus job. Through your work as a peer educator, you likely will gain academic, social, and career-related skills and rewards. For instance, you probably will improve your abilities to make decisions, think through complex issues, and solve a variety of problems. As with others in this position, your communication and leadership skills will grow, as will your feelings of accomplishment and self-confidence. In addition, you will be working cooperatively with other people, including those with differing backgrounds; this will be invaluable in professional settings. Moreover, your work might help you to define your career path. Comments from experienced peer educators underscore the benefits and rewards of this position:

> Being a tutor helped me to organize my thoughts and aided in my interpersonal relations. I've been able to relearn content that I forgot and to improve my study skills.

> After conducting group sessions this past year, I feel much more confident in leading others and am proud that I was able to help so many students.

Furthermore, peer educators' varied job experiences often have a substantial and positive impact on how they view the institution for which they work. As with many peer educators, your work experiences might strengthen the bond you have with your college or university.

> My role as a peer educator has dramatically changed my experience at this university. The interaction with professors has been enlightening, motivating, and confidence building.

> I love working as a tutor. I learn so much from the students I work with. Plus, this job has helped me become a part of the campus community. I can't imagine campus life without it!

In conclusion, as a peer educator, you will experience the powerful impact that you can have on others and the many rewards of meaningful work.

> When I see that look of understanding on a student's face, I consider that a success. I get excited every time someone says, "Oh, my gosh; <u>now</u> I see!"

> One particular topic—aerobic respiration—is very hard for students to understand. I have a special way to present the topic so that everyone understands. I feel like I can see the light bulbs switching on. Wow—it amazes me that I can have that kind of power and effect!

> As I leave this position, I realize what an incredible experience it has been. Although frustrating at times, being an SI leader has been enjoyable and rewarding. I am so thankful for this opportunity.

ACTIVITY 1.2

INTERVIEWING

Interview an experienced peer educator, using the following questions. Share your interview answers with others who are training for peer educator positions.

1. Describe examples of how your experiences working as a peer educator have affected your:
   - Intellectual abilities or academic performance.
   - Personal and leadership skills.
   - Social and communication skills.
   - Professional or workplace skills.

2. In what ways have your experiences as a peer educator influenced your career decisions, options for graduate school, or other aspects of your future?

3. Describe one experience as a peer educator that stands out in your mind. Why is this incidence significant to you?

Learning Strategy: Managing Your Time

Managing one's time is a fundamental element of developing into a responsible, successful, adultlike learner. As a peer educator, you will work with many students, especially first-year students, who have little experience with how to structure their days and balance academic and leisure activities effectively. Poor time management results in missed assignments, sloppy work, procrastination, rushed activities, and a great deal of stress. In your sessions, emphasize to students the importance of organizing their time, including the use of daily to-do lists, weekly schedules, and semester calendars, either written or electronic.

ASSESS YOUR TIME MANAGEMENT SKILLS

For each item, A–L, place an "x" in the column that most accurately describes you.

FIGURE 1.3 Time management assessment

	1 Rarely	2 Sometimes	3 Usually	4 Always
A. I remember what assignments are due for each course each week.				
B. I get adequate amount of sleep each night (usually 7–9 hours).				
C. I have assignments, quiz and test dates, appointments, meetings, work hours, and activities written in a central location.				
D. I know important semester dates: class starting and ending dates; semester breaks; midterm and final exam periods; and deadlines for add/drop, course withdrawal, financial aid, and payment of bills.				
E. I take breaks when studying and then get back to work immediately.				
F. I prioritize what I need to accomplish each day.				
G. I know when and where my classes meet; available times to eat, exercise, and do chores; work hours; and open time slots for study.				
H. Once I start a task, I complete it.				
I. I am not confused about course responsibilities and requirements.				
J. I complete assignments, papers, and projects in a timely manner.				
K. I feel in control of how I manage my time.				
L. I successfully balance academic requirements, personal responsibilities, and leisure activities.				
Column totals:				
Total score:				

ACTIVITY 1.3 *Continued*

DIRECTIONS FOR SCORING

Column totals. For each column, add the number of x's. Then, multiply this sum by the number at the top of the column. Write your total for each of the four columns.

Total score. Add the four column totals. Write this sum beside "Total score."

Interpreting your score. Your total score will be between 12 and 48. Your total score generally represents how adept and self-directed you are about managing your time.

FIGURE 1.4 Interpreting your time-management score

A total score of	Represents
36–48	You skillfully manage your time. What are three strategies that help you to manage your time effectively? Share your approaches with your peers, especially those scoring between 12 and 35.
24–35	You have *some*, but not enough, control over your time. You need to adjust and add different time-management strategies.
12–23	You do *not* have control of your time. To accomplish more while lowering your stress, implement new time-management strategies. Consider seeking assistance from peers, an advisor, or learning assistance center.

STRATEGIES FOR IMPROVING TIME MANAGEMENT

Refer to the items in A–L on the time-management assessment; pay attention to items that you marked "rarely" or "sometimes" (columns one and two). Next, examine the following recommended strategies associated with these items.

1. Use a calendar to keep track of semester dates and deadlines. → Items C, D, K, L

2. Make a daily list—either written or electronic—of what you want to accomplish. Prioritize the tasks. After completing a task, cross it off. → Items A, B, E, F, H, I, J, K, L

3. Use a planner to organize and keep track of your academic, personal, and social obligations and responsibilities. → Items A, B, C, D, E, F, G, I, J, K, L

4. Use a weekly block schedule to create a visual overview of committed and available time each week. Begin by filling in classes, labs, work, and other commitments. Then, find blocks of time available for personal activities (eat, sleep, exercise, family responsibilities, and chores) and social or leisure activities. → Items B, E, G, J, K, L

SETTING GOALS

Personal goals provide a means by which to change or refine behaviors and are useful when working with students over a period of time. As you read through chapters in this text, create goals that will increase your proficiency in the dual roles of college student and peer educator. When creating a personal goal, you are much more likely to be successful if you incorporate these seven elements:

1. **Be specific about what you will accomplish.** The most common error is for students to make very general goal statements, which are ineffective when changing behaviors. For example, the goal "I will add more study time" is very broad—this student could study ten added minutes and still complete the goal!

2. **Be realistic about your goal.** If you identify a goal that you are unlikely to accomplish, you are setting yourself up for failure. For instance, the student who created the goal "I will study 90 minutes in the library every evening" probably will *not* study in the library Friday and Saturday evenings. Be honest with yourself; create a practical goal that you likely can complete.

3. **Have a time constraint.** Develop a goal with a beginning and ending time. Change happens in small steps; therefore, make your goal short term—a week is a manageable amount of time to try out a goal and works well for peer educators meeting with students on a weekly basis. Here's an example of a goal that is specific, realistic, and with a manageable time constraint:

   "I will review my history lecture notes immediately after the class on M/W/F of this week."

4. **Write down your goal.** You are much more likely to complete your goal if you write it down and keep it in an accessible location. It is too easy to forget about or change goals that are not in print. In peer assistance sessions, direct students to write goals on individual index cards or on a poster board for group goal statements.

5. **Say your goal out loud.** Recite your goal statement to yourself or, better yet, to another person. The act of saying and hearing your goal will help to solidify your intention to follow through. In a peer assistance setting, arrange for students to say their goal aloud to one another in small group sessions or to you in an individual session.

6. **Follow up regarding your level of success.** At the end of the designated time period, immediately evaluate how successful you were. Reflect as to whether you will continue this strategy or if you need to refine or change the strategy. As a peer educator, take the time during sessions for students to evaluate themselves and share commentaries with others.

7. **Include another person.** Tell your goal to another person and let that person know about your level of success. If another person knows about your goal, you are more likely to follow through with your intentions. Given that peer assistance sessions consist of the leader plus one or more students, you readily can incorporate this element into your sessions.

PERSONAL GOAL

If you scored between 12 and 35 on the time-management assessment, you should improve how you manage your time. In particular, make adjustments for those items that you indicated you do "rarely" or "sometimes." To strengthen your time-management skills, create a short-term goal centered on what you will do this week. Complete the following sentence.

This week I will:

Tell another person(s) your goal. Ask that person to evaluate your goal, using the seven elements of an effective goal. Be sure to revisit your goal in one week and assess how effective it was in improving your time management.

1. Is the goal specific?
2. Is the goal realistic?
3. Do you have a time constraint?
4. Is the goal written?
5. Did you say the goal out loud?
6. After one week, did you evaluate your level of success?
7. Who else knows about your goal and your level of success?

Closing

CHECK YOUR UNDERSTANDING

Answer each question below; be specific, descriptive, and thorough. Afterward, compare your current answers with your answers from the opening activity. Are your current answers more accurate and comprehensive than your answers before reading the chapter? Are your current answers clear and comprehensive enough to use as an explanation for someone who has not read the chapter and knows little about the topic? Discuss your answers with other peer educators.

1. What is a peer educator?
2. What is the role of a peer educator?
3. What personal benefits can I expect from working as a peer educator?
4. Summarize your expectations of your peer educator role. List any questions or concerns that you have at this point about the peer educator position.
5. Describe how you can manage your time more effectively.
6. What are the seven key elements of a successful personal goal?

ELEMENTS OF EFFECTIVE PEER-LED SESSIONS

Each text chapter includes components that facilitate learning for you, the reader. These components mirror techniques that facilitate learning for students with whom you work. Therefore, be mindful of assorted chapter features that parallel elements of effective peer-led sessions.

The purpose of this activity is to focus your attention on select features in Chapter 1 that assist with learning. In Figure 1.5, elements of effective peer-led sessions are listed in the left-hand column. Test your understanding of these elements by providing an example from Chapter 1, as indicated in the right-hand column.

FIGURE 1.5 Elements of effective peer-led sessions

Peer educators should	Elements within Chapter 1
Provide an opening activity that previews the session or introduces the topics.	The opening questions focus readers' attention on main topics and highlight what readers should learn in the chapter.
Integrate learning and study strategies within the session.	*Add an example from Chapter 1:*
Provide choices for the learner.	*Add an example from Chapter 1:*
Break down material. Focus on one chunk of information at a time.	*Add an example from Chapter 1:*
Provide application of content.	Readers complete a goal-setting exercise. *Add another example from Chapter 1:*
Include periodic opportunities for students to check their understanding of a topic.	Readers check understanding of content via activities interspersed in chapter. *Add another example from Chapter 1:*
Provide a closing activity that summarizes the session and/or previews the next session.	*Add an example from Chapter 1:*

Suggestions from Experienced Peer Educators

HOW DO YOU INCORPORATE LEARNING AND STUDY STRATEGIES?

Direct students to refer to both the text and class notes for answers to questions. Ask them to highlight answers. This reinforces the importance of reviewing information and finding answers in the sources they already have. Also, this helps focus their attention on examples and terms needed to understand problem areas. (Rick L.)

Before leaving their session, each student has to come up with a goal for using a study strategy. Students write their goal on a sheet of large paper, which I hang in the tutoring room. It's amazing to watch the students read about each other's goals for the week. (Lorenza K.)

I use a combination of activities with the students, reinforcing various learning strategies. For example, students complete worksheets to take home and use as study guides. To help them prepare for the NCLEX, we do sample application questions. We do a lot of practice with reading multiple choice questions and choosing answers since nursing exams are almost always multiple choice. (Breanne D.)

References

Astin, A. (1993). *What matters in college? Four critical years revisited.* San Francisco: Jossey-Bass.

Cabrera, A. F., Crissman, J. L., Bernal, E. M., Amaury, N., Terenzini, P. T., & Pascarella, E. T. (2002). Collaborative learning: Its impact on college students' development and diversity. *Journal of College Student Development, 43*(2), 20–34.

Chickering, A. W., & Reisser, L. (1993). *Education and identity,* 2nd ed. San Francisco: Jossey-Bass.

Higbee, J. L. (1996). *Defining developmental education: A commentary.* Retrieved May 19, 2009, from www.nade.net/documents/Mono96/mono96.7.pdf.

Knowles, M. (1980). *The modern practice of adult education: From pedagogy to andragogy,* 2nd ed. New York: Cambridge Books.

Knowles, M. (1992). Applying principles of adult learning in conference presentations. *Adult Learning, 4*(1), 12.

CHAPTER 2

Promoting Active Learning

OPENING: FOCUS QUESTIONS

The following questions represent the learning objectives of this chapter, that is, content that the author expects the reader to understand upon completion of this chapter. Similarly, place questions on the board or on a sheet of paper to focus students' attention on the topics, purpose, and expectations for your academic support session.

1. What is active learning? Describe at least three ways that a student learns actively.
2. Describe the key elements of the information processing model of learning.
3. What is meant by the term *cognitive learning style*? Describe your cognitive learning style.
4. Why is recognition of cognitive style important in academic assistance sessions?
5. How can you incorporate learning styles into your peer-led sessions?

As a comprehension check at the end of this chapter, you will be directed to provide detailed answers to each question. Likewise, at the end of your peer-led sessions, ensure that students are able to answer the opening questions both completely and correctly.

Tell me and I'll forget, show me and I may remember, involve me and I will understand.

— Chinese proverb

Active Learning

Active learning refers to the behaviors and attitudes associated with self-directed, self-motivated, and independent learning—in other words, andragogical learning (as described in Chapter 1). Active learners take the initiative to ask questions, to select appropriate learning and study strategies, and to monitor their levels of success.

The role of a peer educator is to assist students with how to learn, including how to understand and remember difficult content. Therefore, you should integrate a variety of active learning techniques within your sessions. In various chapters, you will be identifying and applying active-learning strategies for yourself so that you ultimately can promote similar strategies for the students with whom you work.

ACTIVITY 2.1

PROMOTING ACTIVE LEARNING

Even though you promote and model the attitudes and behaviors associated with active, successful learning, inevitably you will encounter students who put forth minimal effort and are steadfast in their passive approach toward academics. With the goal to merely "get by" in school, some students might put pressure on you to tell them the correct answers or give them copies of your class notes. How do you encourage the passive students to adopt a more active approach toward their learning?

Refer to Figure 2.1. Compose an appropriate peer educator response for each comment from students. Indicate what the peer educator can *say* or *do* to promote active learning. Then, share your responses with other peer educators, and add two more responses from others.

FIGURE 2.1 Promoting active learning

Comment from student	Appropriate responses from peer educator
Please give me the answers to the worksheet items.	1.
	2.
	3.
I'm just trying to get a "D" on the test so that I pass the course.	1.
	2.
	3.
I slept in and missed class. Can you teach me this information?	1.
	2.
	3.

Down time. *Down time* is a chunk of time in a session during which a student is neither working nor thinking and, therefore, can be totally passive. Because students complete work at differing paces, down time is most prevalent in group sessions. In one-on-one tutorial sessions, down time most often occurs when the tutor talks more than necessary, which causes the student to tune out and lose attention. Needless to say, students should experience as little down time as possible in your sessions.

To reduce down time, give students explicit time limits for an activity, which helps students judge how to pace their work. Also, you need not wait for all students to complete an activity before moving on to another whole-group activity. When the first group completes an activity, begin to review content and check answers as a whole group. Then, call on members of the first group to answer the questions or help solve the problems that others have not begun. Or divide up the questions so that groups are tackling fewer questions or problems.

Eliminating down time requires advanced planning. Be prepared to direct the students who finish first to the next step or another activity. As examples, students who finish early can:

- Help other students who are still working.
- Complete an additional activity or set of problems.
- Do a backup activity, such as an extra worksheet, lab sheet, or end-of-chapter questions.
- Add to an ongoing bank of potential test questions, which can be used for the pre-exam review session.
- Write answers, steps, or reasons on the board.
- Exchange, critique, or check each other's work.
- Begin homework or work on other requirements for the course.
- Review and highlight class notes, outline a text chapter, make study cards, or apply other recommended study strategies for the course.

How Learning Occurs

INFORMATION PROCESSING MODEL

How an individual understands and remembers new information is explained by way of a theoretical model termed *information processing*. According to this model, learning involves a three-stage progression:

Stage I: A person receives or takes in the information.

Stage II: A person sorts through, organizes, and modifies the information so that it makes sense to him or her.

Stage III: A person stores the information into long-term memory, retrieving it when needed.

Peer educators can intervene in this three-stage process by showing students strategies that maximize their learning of difficult course work. Many college students, especially first-year students, have little experience with such strategies.

Stage I: Introduce students to recommended approaches for receiving information during class. Also, demonstrate ways that students can take in information from their out-of-class readings and assignments. Examples of strategies for stage I include:

- Become familiar with the topic by skimming the chapter before class.
- Have your text open during class in order to highlight topics and terms that the instructor stresses.
- If you are confused during class, ask the instructor for clarification and examples.
- Reduce external and internal distractions. This will increase your concentration when reading and completing assignments.
- When the instructor stresses important topics, keep track of corresponding pages in the textbook. Reread these pages after class; add specific explanations and examples in your class notes.

Stage II: This stage is crucial for understanding unfamiliar, complex subject matter. Thus, intentionally utilize a range of strategies in your sessions that help students make sense of course content. Examples of learning techniques for stage II include:

- Summaries that paraphrase key ideas.
- Charts that categorize content.
- Mind maps that show hierarchies and link ideas.
- Flowcharts that illustrate procedures and steps.

Stage III: Show students techniques that help them retain information for future use, such as an upcoming quiz or exam. Examples of learning strategies for stage III include:

- Practice tests to rehearse content.
- Case studies to apply information.
- Lab scenarios to transfer content.
- Reciting out loud as you review material.

In conclusion, as a peer educator, be prepared to demonstrate and recommend a range of strategies that aid students with maximizing their understanding and retention of difficult content. As students transfer these strategies to their course work, they will develop into increasingly successful, confident, and independent learners.

INFORMATION PROCESSING AND LEARNING STRATEGIES

Refer to Figure 2.2. The left-hand column distinguishes three key sources of new information for students in a typical college course—information received in the class, information received when reading the textbook or assignments, and information received when studying and preparing for a quiz or exam. Think about the learning strategies and study habits that you have developed

FIGURE 2.2 Information processing stages and learning strategies

Information Processing Model → / Source of information ↓	Stage I What do you do to take in accurate and complete information?	Stage II What do you do to sort through, organize, and modify information so that it makes sense to you?	Stage III What do you do to store and retain information for a test or assignment?
In class	*Before class, skim notes from previous class session.*	*After class, add material from textbook to class notes.*	*Go through all notes weekly until test.*
Reading assignments			
Preparing for tests			

as a college student. For each information source, add at least two strategies that you have used in each stage. An example is provided for in-class information.

Afterward, add more strategies as you share and discuss this exercise with other peer educators.

Information processing model in a peer-led session. The following is an example of how the three-stage information processing model is applied in a peer-led session:

1. *The learner receives or takes in information* → The student, Chandra, listens to a lecture and writes notes.

   - In the tutorial session, the peer educator asks Chandra to describe how she listens and takes notes during class. Looking at Chandra's notes, the peer educator makes several suggestions, including writing in pen, not pencil; using phrases, not whole sentences; writing on one side of the paper; and leaving space to add information after class. To illustrate these points, the peer educator shows notes he has taken in various courses. Chandra agrees to try these suggestions and bring her new notes to next week's tutorial session.

2. *The learner sorts through, organizes, and modifies the information so that it makes sense* → Chandra quickly reviews her notes right before the next class.

   - The peer educator stresses the importance of going through class notes shortly after class while the information is still fresh in Chandra's mind. The peer educator suggests identifying important terms, saying them out loud, highlighting them in the notes, and adding personal examples. Also, when Chandra encounters sections of notes that are unclear, she should add explanations and examples from the textbook. The peer educator asks Chandra to try these techniques during their session together. Afterward, Chandra agrees to continue with these techniques and report back when they meet the following week.

3. *The learner stores the information into long-term memory for future use* → Chandra reviews her notes in preparation for the upcoming test.

   - The peer educator emphasizes the value of rehearsal and repetition as means to strengthen Chandra's memory. The peer educator gives Chandra a practice quiz to complete during their session. Chandra talks out loud as she explains how she answered each practice question. Afterward, Chandra predicts other questions likely to be on the upcoming test. Chandra agrees to practice answering these questions daily until the test next week.

APPLYING THE INFORMATION PROCESSING MODEL

Apply the information processing model using the following scenario. Underneath each stage, indicate how the peer educator can help the student, Jason, improve his approach toward learning.

1. *The learner receives or takes in information* → Jason reads the thirty-page text assignment an hour before class.
   - The peer educator:

2. *The learner sorts through, organizes, and modifies the information so that it makes sense* → Jason highlights the boldfaced headings, subheadings, and terms.
   - The peer educator:

3. *The learner stores the information into long-term memory for future use* → Jason reads through the highlighted headings, subheadings, and terms several days before the test.
   - The peer educator:

Differences in Learning

Though commonalities exist regarding the process and stages of learning, individual differences are present within each stage. Cognitive learning style refers to how individuals prefer to receive, organize, analyze, and store content. Cognitive learning styles are students' favored means of understanding and remembering information and are formed from an intricate combination of early experiences and interactions. Because any cognitive learning style—or preference—is independent of a person's intelligence and abilities, there is no right or wrong style. However, cognitive styles can influence students' choices of which learning strategies to implement for specific subjects and assignments. Your objective as a peer educator is to make students aware of compatible methods of learning new and complex information, as well as how they can adapt to the variety of teaching styles and course requirements they will encounter.

There are a number of ways to assess cognitive learning styles. The two methods presented in this chapter can be used and adapted readily in your work with students.

VISUAL, AUDITORY, AND TACTILE/KINESTHETIC PREFERENCES

One method for assessing cognitive style focuses on visual, auditory, and tactile/kinesthetic modalities of learning. Though people likely use all three of these modalities at various times, most people have preferred modes of learning.

Visual learners prefer to *see* information in their minds when learning. Because visual learners often are competent with identifying connections among ideas, they favor mind maps, flowcharts, graphs, and other visual formats when learning complicated information. In addition, visual learners tend to use color and design in learning situations.

Auditory learners prefer to *hear* information when learning. Auditory learners have a preference for repetitive telling of information, including discussion, debate, talking aloud to themselves, and reciting rhymes. Auditory learners like to listen to and often use tapes, MP3 players, and other forms of recorded material.

Tactile/kinesthetic learners prefer to learn by *touching* and *doing*. They favor experiential learning and physical, hands-on tasks, including lab work, field trips, role playing, dramatizing, and demonstration of subject matter. In addition, tactile/kinesthetic learners prefer media containing real-life scenarios, such as videos, podcasts, and computer simulations. Tactile/kinesthetic learners like to use case studies, examples, and personal analogies to understand new and complex material.

Several items to be mindful of regarding visual, auditory, and tactile/kinesthetic preferences:

- Practically *all* students, even those with strong visual or auditory preferences, strengthen their learning through application and practice.
- No one modality is superior to others.
- Most adult learners rely on two or three modalities in a learning situation and tend to incorporate multiple strategies in schoolwork. Because an increased use of learning strategies is related to increased understanding and remembering of content, students using a combination of modalities and strategies often have an advantage in learning.

ACTIVITY 2.4

ASSESSING LEARNING MODALITIES

Based on the strategies that you implement regularly, do you tend to use one modality over the others? Or would you classify yourself as being multimodal? For an estimate of your dominant learning modalities, complete Figure 2.3.

Continued

ACTIVITY 2.4 *Continued*

FIGURE 2.3 Assessing learning modalities

Directions. Place an "x" beside a strategy if *it describes you on a regular basis.* Then, total the number of x's for each modality.

Visual Learning
— 1. You like instructors to use the board or overhead screen and to provide a visual outline or PowerPoint of subjects to be covered.
— 2. You like the use of videos, films, or maps in a classroom.
— 3. You make frequent use of color coding new information, including highlighters, different colored pens, or colored sticky notes.
— 4. You prefer information to be presented in charts, diagrams, pictures, or illustrations.
— 5. To understand what you read, you mark the margins of pages, use symbols and numbers, and highlight key words or phrases.
— 6. You create charts, tables, or spreadsheets to organize information.
— 7. You "see" information in your mind in order to remember it.
— 8. You like to use study cards to remember key points and terms.
— 9. You use drawings, pictures, and other designs to help remember information.
— 10. You create mind maps to illustrate important and complicated concepts.

Auditory Learning
— 1. You like instructors to present information via lecture in order to hear explanations.
— 2. You like to participate in class discussions.
— 3. You prefer to listen to others and talk about information.
— 4. You read out loud in order to understand complex ideas.
— 5. You "hear" information in order to remember it.
— 6. You like to use books on tape.
— 7. Talking out loud helps you understand and remember information.
— 8. You record and listen to notes in order to remember key points.
— 9. You prefer to study with others.
— 10. You benefit from obtaining information from CDs, podcasts, or audiotapes.

Tactile/Kinesthetic Learning
— 1. You learn best when physically engaged in a hands-on activity.
— 2. You like instructors who use demonstrations in the classroom.
— 3. You do not prefer the traditional means of learning—lectures in class and readings out of class.
— 4. You like experiential learning, including labs, fieldwork, and projects.
— 5. You prefer that information be presented as a physical activity or materials that you can work with, feel, and manipulate.
— 6. You learn more when given a chunk of information at a time, as opposed to a whole unit, entire chapter, or packet of material.

— 7. You like to move about when you are reading or studying.
— 8. To help you understand and remember information, you jot down key words, draw illustrations, maneuver flash cards, or create a model.
— 9. To learn new and complex information, you like to spend time out of the classroom doing fieldwork, working in a lab, or practicing a procedure.
— 10. You often use large square graph paper to assist in creating charts and diagrams that illustrate key concepts.

Totals: Visual _____   Auditory _____   Tactile/Kinesthetic _____

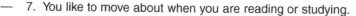

ACTIVITY 2.5

ANALYZING LEARNING MODALITIES

Part I. Identify each of the strategies you listed in Figure 2.2, p. 18 as being visual (v), auditory (a), tactile/kinesthetic (t/k), or a combination of two or more modalities.

Part II. Refer to Figure 2.4, p. 24. Six learning modalities are listed in the far left column. For each lettered column, complete the following:

A. Identify each modality as being visual (v), auditory (a), and/or tactile/kinesthetic (t/k).

B. Place an "x" in the box beside each modality primarily associated with *receiving information.*

C. Place an "x" in the box beside each modality primarily associated with *transmitting information.*

D. Place an "x" in the box beside each modality associated with *passive learning.*

E. Place an "x" in the box beside each modality associated with *active learning.*

Part III. In one to two paragraphs, summarize the chart by answering these questions: How do you interpret the distribution of x's? What is the central principle of this chart? What does this mean to you in your work as a peer educator?

Part IV. Answer these questions:

1. For the typical college course, which modalities do students most often use *in class*? Explain.

Continued

ACTIVITY 2.5 *Continued*

2. For the typical college course, which modalities do students most often use to complete *out-of-class assignments*? Explain.

3. For the typical college course, which modalities do students most often use to *prepare for a test*? Explain.

FIGURE 2.4 Analyzing learning modalities

Modality	A. visual auditory tactile/kinesthetic	B. Receives information	C. Transmits information	D. Passive learning	E. Active learning
see					
listen					
talk					
read					
write					
manipulate					

To increase students' understanding and retention of course content, peer educators should incorporate plenty of activities for which students use the expressive modalities: talking, writing, and manipulating. These modalities are associated with stages II and III of the information processing model.

On the other hand, reading, listening, and seeing are connected to input of information and are associated with stage I of the information processing model. These receptive modalities are more passive means of learning. One of your goals as a peer educator is to show students how to incorporate active modalities (talking, writing, and manipulating) when listening in class and reading assignments.

Furthermore, in your sessions, students should be *speaking* (talking through solutions, verbalizing problems, answering questions, discussing issues, explaining), as well as *writing* and *manipulating* (rearranging ideas, categorizing topics, summarizing content, building a model, replicating a process, showing steps, devising text questions, illustrating a concept, solving problems, assessing progress). These and similar activities involve your students directly in the learning process.

On a final note, be attentive to who is doing most of the talking and writing/typing in your sessions—is it you or the student(s) with whom you are working? It is easy for peer educators to slip into the role of lecturers who give information. Be mindful and patient during your session; remember that students should be doing the majority of talking, writing, working, and, ultimately, learning. Your role as peer educator is to plan ahead, direct activities, ask questions, demonstrate strategies, and, in similar ways, guide the students' learning. As Mina Shaughnessy, a respected writing instructor, noted: "To do things for the student that he can do for himself is not generosity but impatience."

PERSONALITY TYPE

Another method for assessing cognitive style is based on the assumption that differences in personality help to explain the differences in how students learn. Underlying Swiss psychiatrist Carl Jung's theory of psychological type are sixteen predictable patterns of personality, termed "types." To measure personality types, Katharine Cook Briggs and Isabel Briggs Myers (1998) developed the Myers–Briggs Type Indicator personality inventory to assess individuals' preferred means of perceiving and organizing information, as defined by four dimensions:

- Extraversion (E) or Introversion (I)
- Sensing (S) or Intuition (N)
- Thinking (T) or Feeling (F)
- Judging (J) or Perceiving (P)

ACTIVITY 2.6

ASSESSMENT

Before reading an explanation of each dimension, evaluate your preferred patterns of thinking and learning. If you do not have access to the Myers–Briggs Type Indicator inventory, complete the informal assessment provided in Figure 2.5.

Directions. In a *learning situation*, which pattern describes you better? For each row in Figure 2.5, place an "x" in the box that describes you *more often when learning new content and studying for exams*. Then total your "x's" for each of the four dimensions.

FIGURE 2.5 Thinking about mental habits

Extraversion (E)	or	Introversion (I)
❑ I prefer action and variety.		❑ I prefer quiet and time to consider things.
❑ I prefer to do mental work by talking to people.		❑ I prefer to do mental work privately before talking.
❑ I act quickly, sometimes without much reflection.		❑ I prefer to understand something before trying it.
❑ I like to see how other people do a task and to see results.		❑ I prefer to understand the idea of a task and to work alone or with just a few people.
❑ I want to know what other people expect of me.		❑ I prefer setting my own standards.
__ Total for "E"		__ Total for "I"
Sensing (S)	**or**	**Intuition (N)**
❑ I usually pay most attention to experience and what something is.		❑ I usually pay most attention to the meanings of facts and how they fit together.

Continued

ACTIVITY 2.6 *Continued*

❏ I prefer to use my eyes, ears, and other senses to find out what is happening.	❏ I prefer to use my imagination to come up with new ways and possibilities to do things.
❏ I dislike new problems unless I've had prior experiences showing how to solve them.	❏ I like solving new problems. I dislike doing the same thing over and over.
❏ I enjoy using skills already learned more than learning new skills.	❏ I enjoy learning new skills more than practicing old skills.
❏ I am patient with details but impatient when the details become complicated.	❏ I am impatient with details but don't mind complicated situations.
___ Total for "S"	___ Total for "N"

Thinking (T)	or	Feeling (F)
❏ I prefer to use logic when making decisions.	❏ I prefer to use personal feelings and values when making decisions.
❏ I want to be treated with justice and fair play.	❏ I like praise and like to please other people, even in small matters.
❏ I may neglect and hurt other people's feelings without knowing it.	❏ I am usually very aware of other people's feelings.
❏ I give more attention to ideas or things, rather than to human relationships.	❏ I can predict how others will feel.
❏ I can get along with little harmony among people.	❏ I prefer harmony among people and feel unsettled by arguments and conflicts.
___ Total for "T"	___ Total for "F"

Judging (J)	or	Perceiving (P)
❏ I like to make a plan, to have things settled and decided ahead of time.	❏ I like to stay flexible and avoid fixed plans.
❏ I prefer to make things come out the way they ought to be.	❏ I deal easily with unplanned and unexpected happenings.
❏ I prefer to finish one project before starting another.	❏ I like to start many projects, though I may have trouble finishing them all.
❏ I usually have my mind made up.	❏ I usually am looking for new information.
❏ I may decide things too quickly.	❏ I may decide things too slowly.
❏ I want to be right.	❏ I want to miss nothing.
❏ I live by standards and schedules that are not easily changed.	❏ I live by making changes to deal with problems as they come along.
___ Total for "J"	___ Total for "P"

Source: Lawrence, G.D. (1993). *People types and tiger stripes*, 3rd ed. Gainesville, FL: Center for Applications of Psychological Type. Used with permission. This exercise is NOT a type indicator, nor does it replicate the Myers-Briggs Type Indicator® personality inventory, which is a validated instrument. Myers-Briggs Type Indicator, Myers-Briggs, and MBTI are trademarks or registered trademarks of the Myers-Briggs Type Indicator Trust in the United States and other countries.

Scoring. For each dimension, the column with the highest number of "x's" represents your dominant preference. Write the four letters that received the highest total for each dimension (such as, "INFP" or "ENTJ"): _____.

Keep in mind that:

- The higher the number, the stronger the preference. For instance, a total of 5 on any dimension represents a more dominant preference than does a total of 3.
- If the difference between two totals is only 1 point, you may not have a clear-cut preference within that dimension. For example, suppose you have a total of 3 for Extraversion and a total of 2 for Introversion. For this dimension, you show traits of both, with Extraversion possibly your main preference.
- Your four letters represent an approximation of your type. The standardized version of the Myers-Briggs Type Indicator® personality inventory is a much more reliable and valid measure of personality type than is this informal exercise.
- Everyone exhibits characteristics of each cognitive type in various situations. The purpose of this exercise is for you to identify your dominant preference when learning new and complex information and then to use this information to tailor techniques for study, both for you and for your students.

Description of the Dimensions

Each dimension describes an element of how a person prefers to take in, organize, and retain information, that is, a person's information processing habits as a reflection of personality. Furthermore, each dimension represents a continuum with people at each extreme and a larger percentage of the population falling at various locations between. For instance, people who are strongly extraverted or strongly introverted are at either end of that continuum, with the majority of people somewhere in between.

E—Extraversion refers to individuals who generally are comfortable in social settings and enjoy reaching out to other people. Extraverted students are oriented to the outside world and like to talk and interact with others. Extraverted students often prefer action and movement when learning.

I—Introversion refers to individuals who are oriented to ideas and reflection. Introverted students generally are most comfortable working quietly alone, with time to think about and process information.

S—Sensing refers to individuals who favor specific, concrete, reality-based learning. Sensing students tend to be careful with details and facts and prefer sequential, step-by-step circumstances. Sensing students prefer relevant, hands-on, experiential activities.

N—Intuition refers to individuals who favor abstractions and are inspired by possibilities and complex situations. Intuitive students tend to see the "big picture" and respond positively to challenges, such as making associations among ideas, figuring out solutions, and deciphering new problems. Intuitive students prefer inferential, conceptual learning activities.

T—Thinking refers to individuals who are analytical, logical, and even impersonal. Thinking individuals prefer to objectively weigh the pros and cons when making decisions. Thinking students tend to be purposeful and orderly when learning and like to fulfill specific goals and objectives.

F—Feeling refers to individuals who are aware of other people's feelings and who value harmony among people. Feeling individuals often consider other people when making decisions. Feeling students prefer a learning setting that includes personal rapport, support, and feedback from others.

J—Judging refers to individuals who prefer organization, planning, and consistency and avoid impromptu, unpredictable situations. Judging students rely on clear-cut structure and well-defined expectations when learning. Judging students tend to get things done in an orderly manner.

P—Perceiving refers to individuals who prefer new and different situations and often are curious, spontaneous, and flexible. Perceiving students tend to welcome new challenges and avoid structured, detailed assignments. Perceiving students are resourceful, especially when confronted with last-minute changes.

ACTIVITY 2.7

REFLECTING

Refer back to your four-letter type and write your answers to the following: Having read the description of each dimension, consider whether your combination is accurate for you. Think about how you approach learning and studying. In which ways does your four-letter type accurately describe you? If another combination more accurately describes you, write that combination and the reason for switching to this other four-letter type.

ACTIVITY 2.8

LEARNING PREFERENCES AND LEARNING STRATEGIES

1. Consider which learning and study strategies you might recommend to a student based on his or her cognitive learning type. First, review the characteristics associated with each type (Figure 2.5, p. 25). Then, refer to Figure 2.6. For each dimension, read the examples provided. Then, think of two to three additional strategies. If possible, brainstorm with other peer educators to complete this activity.

2. To the right of each strategy listed in your chart, indicate if that strategy favors visual (v), auditory (a), and/or tactile/kinesthetic (t/k) modalities.

FIGURE 2.6 Cognitive style and learning strategies

Extraversion	• Go to group study, review, or tutorial sessions each week. Be sure to write the days and times in your planner. • Teach content to other people to help reinforce what you do or do not know.
Introversion	• Study in a location free of noise and distractions from other people. • Provide adequate time after class to review and think about your class notes.
Sensing	• Study for difficult, complicated courses when you feel the freshest. • Because essay test items can be your weakness, practice how to best answer them.
Intuition	• Read to discover new ideas. • Because you like to consider how ideas are related, summarize material using mind maps and diagrams.
Thinking	• Go to your instructor or a tutor when you need help with course work (someone with whom you don't socialize).
Feeling	• Surround yourself with people who are supportive of your academic endeavors.
Judging	• Create a priority list each day. Include academic assignments and personal responsibilities. • Because you may get anxious when encountering unexpected test questions, practice stress-reduction techniques
Perceiving	• Be alert to your tendency to procrastinate on assignments. Write down when you will do schoolwork. Break large assignments into steps. • Ask questions to keep the subject interesting.

Closing

ACTIVITY 2.9

HOW DO *YOU* LEARN BEST?

Create a visual summary explaining your cognitive styles and approaches of learning. Incorporate the following elements within your summary:

• Results of your four-letter learning type (Figure 2.5), as well as your preferences for visual, auditory, tactile/kinesthetic modalities (Figure 2.3).
• Choices and examples of your strategies for learning.

Continued

ACTIVITY 2.9 *Continued*

Select a medium that allows you to be creative yet thoughtful in the design and content of your summary. One option is to use poster board or a sturdy canvas and add colorful lettering, pictures, illustrations, designs, or collages that represent your learning styles and strategies. Or you might choose to construct a PowerPoint presentation, video, or a performance piece.

When finished, show and explain your summary to others in your class. If possible, display it so that the students you work with can see how *you* learn best.

ACTIVITY 2.10

CHECKING FOR UNDERSTANDING

Write a detailed answer for each question or statement below. Compare and contrast with other peer educators' answers. As needed, add and revise your answers to make them complete, accurate, and clear.

1. What is active learning? Describe at least three ways that a student learns actively.

2. Describe the key elements of the information processing model of learning.

3. What is meant by the term *cognitive learning style*? Describe your cognitive learning style.

4. Why is recognition of cognitive style important in academic assistance sessions?

5. How can you incorporate learning styles into your peer-led sessions?

ACTIVITY 2.11

APPLYING

Reread the proverb at the beginning of the chapter: "Tell me and I'll forget, show me and I may remember, involve me and I will understand." As a peer educator, how can you involve students in the learning process? Describe three methods for your subject area.

1.

2.

3.

Suggestions from Experienced Peer Educators

HOW DO YOU INCREASE ACTIVE PARTICIPATION?

Students make up a question about the lesson on a note card, then students exchange note cards and answer each others' questions. (Jennie L.)

Put 3–5 questions, focusing on main points from notes and reading, on the board—the first few I make up, the last few I get from students. Pairs of students write and explain their answers on the board. The other students make corrections, as needed. (Kylie L.)

Quiz students on information, using real-life situations that are as humorous as possible. (Sam G.)

Make the students comfortable about making mistakes, with statements such as: "Good try, however . . . ." "I think the professor was looking for a slightly different answer. Does anyone else have a suggestion?" (Brenda M.)

Have an informal roundtable discussion. First, students brainstorm about questions they have on readings. Then, others tell information they know about the topic. (Jerrell M.)

 Pass the chalk or marker around so each student goes to the board and becomes more actively involved in the session. (Lisa S.)

References

Arendale, D. (2002). *Supplemental instruction study strategies: Using the information processing model.* Retrieved July 7, 2005, from www.iup.edu/lec/AcadAssist/SI/IPM-relatedSIstrategies[1].doc.

Bernstein, S. N. Ed. (2007). *Teaching developmental writing: Background readings*, 3rd ed. New York: Bedford, p. 12.

Briggs, K. C. & Myers, I. B. (1998). *Myers-Briggs Type Indicator*, Form M. Palo Alto, CA: Consulting Psychologists Press, Inc. *Myers-Briggs Type Indicator, Myers Briggs*, and *MBTI* are trademarks or registered trademarks of the Myers-Briggs Type Indicator Trust in the United States and other countries.

Lawrence, G. D. (1993). Exercise: Thinking about mental habits. *People Types and Tiger Stripes*, 3rd ed. (pp. 2–4) Gainesville, FL: Center for Applications of Psychological Type.

CHAPTER 3

Incorporating Critical Thinking and Questioning Skills

OPENING: READING TEXTBOOKS

It is not uncommon for students to avoid reading textbook chapters, which often they describe as being difficult and boring. As a peer educator, introduce strategies that will help students to read text material in an effective yet efficient manner. Methods to help students understand and remember text information (hard copy and online) generally consist of four elements. In your sessions, be sure to demonstrate, practice, and reinforce these elements using the assigned reading materials for the targeted course.

1. **Preview the assignment.** The purpose of previewing is to familiarize yourself with the content before reading it. Knowing what to expect in a reading assignment helps focus your attention and increase your interest in the subject matter. Encourage students to preview a chapter, article, or other assignment before they begin to read.

2. **Break up your reading; check your understanding.** After reading a section in the chapter or article, stop and check your comprehension. A simple yet effective comprehension check is to

Questions are the catalyst for learning.

— Michael Wesch, assistant professor of cultural anthropology, Kansas State University

ask yourself questions about what you just read. Or see if you can answer the ready-made questions within the chapter. If you don't understand the material, reread it before moving on to the next section.

3. **Create a study guide.** The purpose of a study guide is to help you select, organize, understand, and remember important ideas that you likely will need to know for an upcoming exam, discussion, paper, or project. Study guides can be typed or written and consist of varying formats: developing and answering questions; highlighting and annotating text pages; outlining; making study cards; and creating visual summaries, such as charts, concept maps, and diagrams.

4. **Review periodically.** Use your study guide as a tool for review and reinforcement. Look over the material weekly, talking out loud to yourself. As you review your study guide, add clarifying information from your lecture notes and anticipate potential test questions.

ACTIVITY 3.1

PRACTICE PREVIEWING

Answer the following questions prior to reading the remainder of this chapter. In your sessions, use similar questions when students practice previewing targeted reading assignments.

1. How often do you preview a chapter or reading assignment? (Consider both hard copy and online assignments.)

2. What are the parts or elements of a chapter that you should look at when previewing it?

3. How would you respond to the student who says previewing is a waste of time?

4. Give yourself one minute to preview this chapter. Afterward, say out loud what you found out about the chapter. Mention ideas and topics covered, as well as features, layout, and difficulty level of the chapter.

5. What are your plans for reading the chapter? How much time do you anticipate needing to read adequately? When and where will you be reading the chapter? Will you be highlighting and marking pages or creating another type of study guide?

6. Write one benefit you derived from previewing this chapter.

Introduction

Learning entails more than just memorizing details. True learning implies a deeper level of understanding that involves analysis, evaluation, and application of information. Unfortunately, many students are accustomed only to memorizing terms and details that they expect to rehash on an exam. In your peer educator role, you can help students go beyond such routine, surface-level learning. By implementing three key strategies in your sessions, you can guide students to gain a deeper understanding of subject matter.

TALK OUT LOUD

Talking through subject matter during peer-led sessions is based on a model called *cognitive process instruction* (Lochhead & Clement, 1979). Central to this model is that both the student and the peer educator talk out loud as they work their way through content.

Throughout a session, students verbalize what they understand, or think they understand, as well as what they are confused about (Burmeister, 1996). Talking out loud provides students with opportunities to:

- Recognize and correct mistakes.
- Uncover gaps in knowledge and errors in reasoning.
- Reveal areas that they are uncertain about.
- Confirm procedures and thought patterns that are correct and appropriate.
- Validate successful learning strategies while fine-tuning weaker strategies.

Meanwhile, the peer educator hears how students are approaching content and can guide their thinking by interjecting appropriate questions and direction, such as: *Why did you add this? How did you get this conclusion? What do you think comes next? Go back and check your work.*

Similarly, by voicing their thought processes, peer educators model how to reach a conclusion, how to solve a problem, how to arrive at an answer, and how to proceed when experiencing difficulties. Just as students learn how to revise and rewrite papers, they learn how to rethink and rework information in order to figure out a solution or conclusion. Cognitive process instruction emphasizes the steps and re-steps required of deeper-level thinking. Both the leader and the students become accustomed to verbally sharing what they did, how they did it, and why they did it. For students, this verbal sharing demystifies the process of thinking through difficult problems, breaking down complicated material, and understanding challenging subject matter.

ACTIVITY 3.2

PRACTICE COGNITIVE PROCESS INSTRUCTION

Practice applying the principles of cognitive process instruction. Use situations that you have encountered in your sessions or observed in other peer educators' sessions, or use the sample scenarios in the Instructor's Manual for this text. If possible, involve at least three people—one as the peer educator, one or more as the student, and one as an observer. The observer provides a critique of the mini-session, using the answers to these eight questions:

1. How much talking is the peer educator doing? How much talking are students doing?
2. Is the peer educator prompting students to talk about what they do and do not know?
3. Is the peer educator prompting students to actively think about content and problems?
4. Is the peer educator modeling how to approach difficult content or solve a problem?
5. In a group session, is the peer educator engaging *all* students in conversation?
6. Is the peer educator encouraging students to converse among themselves about the topic?
7. Are students reacting to and questioning each others' work?
8. Is the peer educator handling monopolizing, disruptive, or disengaged students effectively?

INCLUDE QUESTIONS

The use of questions is a relatively simple yet important method for developing students' critical-thinking skills. By combining strategic questioning with articulation, you lead students toward a deeper process of thinking. The criteria in Activity 3.3 provide a framework for how to integrate questions in your sessions.

ACTIVITY 3.3

INTEGRATING QUESTIONS IN SESSIONS

Answer the questions that accompany each of the five criteria. The questions prompt you to think about each criterion and are similar to the types of questions to utilize in your sessions.

In your sessions:

1. **Avoid questions that can be answered with a simple "yes" or "no."**
   - Why should you avoid asking yes/no questions?
   - A common yes/no question is *Do you understand this?* What are better questions and directives that prompt students to think actively and

Continued

ACTIVITY 3.3 *Continued*

provide you with feedback regarding students' understanding of a topic? Two samples are provided; add more examples.

1. <u>What are the important ideas? Why are they significant?</u>
2. <u>Solve another, similar problem.</u>
3. _____
4. _____
5. _____

2. **Focus on open-ended question words.**

FIGURE 3.1 Open-ended versus close-ended question words

Open-ended	Close-ended
What?	Who?
Why?	When?
How?	Where?

- What is the difference between open-ended and close-ended question words?
- Why should you focus primarily on open-ended questions in your sessions?

3. **Use *what*, *why*, and *how* questions as a tool for engaging students and jump-starting active learning and deeper-level thinking.** There will be moments in your sessions when students are at a complete loss about a topic, are not talking, or are totally uninvolved. Utilize *what*, *why*, and *how* questions as a means to start the process of thinking and talking.

   For example, a math tutor used the following questions when working with a student who was confused about a homework problem:

   - *What do you think happens next?*
   - *How did you get that answer?*

   Choose a specific topic in the subject that you are tutoring. Then, develop two to three questions to use with students who are having difficulties with the topic.

4. **Follow up with *who*, *when*, and *where* questions, if needed.** For certain subjects and courses, students will need to know people, locations, and dates.

   In the subject that you are tutoring, when do you need to stress *who*, *when*, and *where* questions? Identify two to three situations that would necessitate the use of close-ended questions. For example: a requirement on the student's upcoming test in art history is matching specific artists with corresponding art genres.

5. **Redirect questions back to students whenever possible.** When students ask you a question, reply by asking another question that points them toward discovering an answer. The purpose of answering students' questions with your own question is to guide students' thought processes and mental habits. As explained in the previous chapter, the students, not the peer educator, should be doing most of the talking, thinking, and activity during a session.

The following dialogue between a psychology tutor and student exemplifies how to redirect questions that lead the student toward an understanding of the topic. After reading this portion of the dialogue, indicate how the tutor should respond to the student.

Student (pointing to lecture notes): What is "classical conditioning"?

Tutor: What do you know about it?

Student: Nothing; it is very confusing and doesn't make sense to me at all.

Tutor: What is the definition that you wrote in your class notes?

Student: "A learning situation where a conditioned stimulus paired with an unconditioned stimulus results in an unconditioned response." But what does this mean?

Tutor: What words are you unsure about? Highlight them as you say them.

Student: Conditioned stimulus, unconditioned stimulus, unconditioned response.

Tutor: How can you figure out the meaning of these terms?

Student: Would it be in the glossary?

You indicate how the tutor should respond:

At times it is appropriate for the peer educator to answer students' questions or to explain subject matter. Describe such a situation. Draw from your experiences working with students or observations of other peer educators' sessions.

Think time. *Think time* refers to the period of time that students need to process information and come up with an answer. Don't expect immediate answers to questions. A silent pause following a question allows for reflection by students. The rule of thumb is to wait 30 seconds for students to answer a question. On paper, 30 seconds might seem like a short amount of time; however, in reality, 30 seconds of silence can seem like an eternity. At first, students might be uncomfortable with silent think time. However, they will get accustomed to using the silent moments for processing information and thinking about appropriate answers.

OBSERVING

Do your instructors provide think time in class? Do other peer educators provide think time in their sessions? During the upcoming week, observe a course instructor and a peer educator. Note whether they allow time for students to reflect on and process information. Use a watch or clock with a second hand to take note of how much think time is provided.

INCLUDE HIGHER-LEVEL DIRECTIVES

Benjamin Bloom (1956) categorized cognitive tasks according to six levels, as listed in Figure 3.2. Too often students are accustomed to the lowest level of cognition, simple knowledge or recall of details and information. To achieve success in college course work, students need to perform at the higher levels of cognition. As a peer educator, it is important to employ specific directives—or action words—that guide students' thinking and require them to perform at increasingly sophisticated levels of cognition.

FIGURE 3.2 Bloom's cognitive categories

Bloom's categories	Description	Directive words	Sample activities in academic support sessions
Evaluation level	Judge the value based on clear evidence or select criteria.	Assess, judge, evaluate, measure	Critique each others' answers.
Synthesis level	Put together parts, forming a new structure or pattern.	Create, organize, arrange, propose	Generate practice questions that integrate text and lecture content.
Analysis level	Break down information into parts.	Compare/contrast, relate, categorize, analyze	Create a Venn diagram.
Application level	Use information in new ways.	Predict, demonstrate, solve, apply	Create a flow chart showing how to use a principle.
Comprehension level	Able to grasp meaning.	Explain, simplify, summarize, give examples	Paraphrase the main points of a reading assignment.
Knowledge level	Recall of information.	Restate, describe, define, list	Identify steps in a common procedure.

Examples of suitable directive words are listed in the third column of Figure 3.2. Your goal is to incorporate these words in your verbal directions and responses and to use them in worksheets, practice tests, and other activities in your sessions.

The following points relate to Bloom's cognitive categories:

1. The six categories are not distinct and separate from one another. Instead, the levels often overlap. For instance, "summarize" is listed at the comprehension level in Figure 3.2. However, summarizing can involve synthesis of information, which fits into a higher level of cognition.

2. Peer-led activities often integrate more than one level of cognition. As an example, the peer educator assigns pairs of students a section of the chapter and directs them to outline the most important ideas on a large sheet of paper (knowledge/comprehension). Students then explain the information to the other students (comprehension/analysis levels), and predict what students will need to know for class (application/synthesis levels).

3. Students' time-on-task, effort, and motivation play a major part in the development of critical-thinking skills (Astin, 1999). Though it is important that students spend ample out-of-class time on course work, many students are unfamiliar with what to do during this study time. Therefore, in your sessions, demonstrate and practice fundamental strategies (such as combining/summarizing text and lecture notes, predicting/rehearsing exam questions), which should enhance the effectiveness and efficiency of students' study efforts.

ACTIVITY 3.5

DIRECTIVE WORDS

Match the following words with the appropriate Bloom category in Figure 3.2. Keep in mind that the directive words can be placed appropriately in two or more categories, depending on the context in which they are used.

- Differentiate
- Match
- Rate
- Design
- Paraphrase
- Relate
- Justify

Add. Include one more example in each of the six categories.

Observe. When observing another peer educator, pay particular attention to the use of directive words. What were the most common directive words the peer educator used? What cognitive levels were most apparent in the questions, directions, worksheets, and activities?

Practice. Choose a topic in your subject area. Rehearse how to implement directive words by creating a series of six questions or directions centered on this topic. Start the directives at level one (knowledge) and move upward to level six (evaluation). Afterward, try out your directives with a classmate. Examples of activities that incorporate higher-level thinking skills are provided in the far right column of Figure 3.2. Add other activities to use in your academic support sessions.

ACTIVITY 3.6

CRITIQUING

A continuation of the dialogue between the psychology tutor and student follows. Read and evaluate the tutor's performance: What are the main strengths? (Be specific.) How would you rewrite the script so that the tutor prods the student to think more independently and critically?

Tutor: How can you figure out the meaning of these terms?

Student: Would it be in the glossary?

Tutor: Try it out.

Student: I found "conditioned stimulus" as being neutral and "unconditioned stimulus" as being automatic and "unconditional response" as reflexive.

Tutor: Write this on the board, using the same abbreviations—CS, UCS, UCR—that are in your notes.

[Student writes.]

Tutor: What is an example of each term?

Student: I don't know.

Tutor: What are examples that you find in your notes?

Student: Here's one: the conditioned stimulus (CS)? is a metronome, the unconditioned stimulus (UCS) is meat powder, and the unconditioned response (UCR) is that the dog salivates and drools.

Tutor: Write them on the board beside each term.

[Student writes.]

Tutor: Next, go back to your definition and substitute the examples. Read it aloud to me.

Student: A learning situation where a metronome paired with meat powder results in the dog drooling. The other abbreviation in my notes is CR. What is this?

Tutor: What do you think this stands for? If you can't find it in your notes, take an educated guess.

Student: I found it—conditioned response (CR). What does this mean?

Tutor: Look at your example and think it through. What response is the dog conditioned to do?

Student: Drooling.

Tutor: What causes the drooling?

Student: Hearing the metronome.

Tutor: Why is the dog drooling?

Student: He thinks he will get meat powder.

Tutor: On the board, draw an arrow showing the connection between CS and CR; that is, which one causes the other? Do the same with UCS and UCR.

.... (dialogue continues)

Tutor: Now, come up with another, original example of classical conditioning.

Closing

ACTIVITY 3.7

ANALYZING

Examine this quotation from Harvard professor Rosabeth M. Kanter: "Leaders are more powerful role models when they learn than when they teach" (Holland & Ritvo, 2008, p. 151). How does this quote relate to your role as a peer educator? When have you noticed a peer educator learning during a session? Discuss your answer with other peer educators.

ACTIVITY 3.8

ELEMENTS OF EFFECTIVE PEER-LED SESSIONS

Listed in the left column of Figure 3.3 are elements that facilitate learning and, therefore, should be incorporated in your tutorial or course-based review sessions. These parallel similar elements that facilitate learning for

Continued

ACTIVITY 3.8 *Continued*

readers. As a test of your understanding, provide an example of how each element was incorporated within Chapter 3.

FIGURE 3.3 Elements of effective peer-led sessions

Peer educators should	Examples within Chapter 3
Provide an opening activity that previews the session or introduces topics.	
Integrate learning and study strategies in the session.	
Provide choices for the learner.	
Break down material. Focus on one chunk of information at a time.	
Provide application of content.	
Include periodic opportunities for students to check their understanding of a topic.	
Present information in varied formats that accommodate differing types of learners.	
Provide a comfortable, supportive learning environment.	
Provide a closing activity that summarizes the session and/or previews the next session.	

Suggestions from Experienced Peer Educators

HOW DO YOU ENCOURAGE CRITICAL THINKING?

Never answer a question immediately—always throw it back to the person or group. If no one knows an answer, reduce the question to its simplest form. Continue asking progressively more difficult questions so that students can build on information that they do know in order to discover answers they don't know. (Kate P.)

First, I direct students to explain what they already understand about a particular topic. Then, I pose higher-level questions about the topic. To find answers, students look at their notes and texts and discuss among themselves. I notice that students often add details, examples, and more thorough explanations within their notes. (Jackie H.)

Have the student correct his own mistakes. I always ask the student to explain aloud how he reached the conclusion or answer. This reinforces the need to check the thought process used to answer the question. Often the student will find his own mistakes. (Dejuan W.)

References

Astin, A. W. (1999). Student involvement: A developmental theory for higher education. *Journal of College Student Development, 40(5),* 518–529.

Bloom, B. S. (Ed.) (1956). *Taxonomy of educational objectives, handbook 1: Cognitive domain.* White Plains, NY: Longman.

Burmeister, S. (1996). Supplemental instruction: An interview with Deanna Martin. *Journal of Developmental Education, 20(1),* 22–24, 26.

Corbett, I. M., & Morehead, M. W. (2006, March). *Instructional conversation as a model for tutoring interaction.* West Palm Beach, FL: Teaching Academic Survival Skills Conference.

Holland, T. P., & Ritvo, R. A. (2008). *Nonprofit organizations: Principles and practices.* NY: Columbia University Press.

Lipsky, S. A. (2008). *College study: The essential ingredients,* 2nd ed. Upper Saddle River, NJ: Pearson Prentice Hall Publishers.

Lochhead, J., & Clement, J. (Eds.) (1979). *Cognitive process instruction: Research on teaching thinking skills.* Philadelphia: Franklin Institute Press.

CHAPTER 4

Assessing Students' Learning

OPENING: SELF-ASSESSMENT

1. In two to three sentences, summarize the most useful information that you have learned thus far in your training to become a peer educator.
2. What is a question that you have in respect to your peer educator role, responsibilities, or training?
3. Find the answer to your question. Begin by asking other peer educators, your supervisor, or instructor.
4. What was the purpose of this self-assessment? What information did it provide you, the learner? What information did it provide the instructor?

Arriving at one point is the starting point to another.

— John Dewey, philosopher and educator

Why Assess Students' Learning?

The purpose of academic support sessions is for students to develop approaches for how to learn difficult content. Peer-led sessions should focus on active learning strategies that result in a thorough understanding of content. As the facilitator of the session, how do you know whether students have a thorough understanding of the content?

Informal assessment techniques provide peer educators with immediate information about how much learning has occurred in sessions. The results of these informal assessments will help you plan for sessions and choose which topics to emphasize during the sessions.

Furthermore, informal assessment techniques provide students with direct feedback regarding how well they understand and retain information. Also, students can use these assessment models independently to evaluate their learning. By way of these informal assessments, students practice many recommended learning and study techniques, such as summarizing, reflecting, questioning, paraphrasing, identifying key ideas, and recognizing what they do and do not know.

ACTIVITY 4.1

REFLECTING

Answer this question: When studying, how do you evaluate what you do or do not understand and remember? Describe at least two methods.

How to Assess Students' Learning?

Classroom assessment instruments (Cross & Angelo, 1988) are techniques for obtaining quick, informal, and frequent feedback from students. Originally intended for classroom instructors, these instruments are adapted easily for use in peer-led sessions.

In your role as a peer educator, be cognizant of how much learning has occurred at various times within a session. Take an active role in guiding students' learning by introducing practical assessment strategies. Administer assessment instruments at the beginning, middle, and/or end of a session.

BEGINNING OF SESSION

Assessment at the start of a session provides a baseline of students' knowledge of subject matter and how well they implement key learning strategies. You and the students will obtain a clearer picture of:

- **What students know, don't know, or are unclear about.** A quick assessment at the start provides you with information about content and skills that students do or do not understand, that is, areas to focus on during your time together.

- **Students' preparation level.** Are students implementing appropriate learning strategies, such as reviewing lecture notes and tackling readings, between academic support sessions? An assessment at the opening of a session reinforces your expectations that students complete out-of-class work and come to sessions focused and primed to learn. Furthermore, you will have a better idea of what strategies students are implementing. For instance, students might not realize the effectiveness of creating a Venn diagram to visually summarize similarities and differences.

The opening exercise of this chapter is an example of an informal assessment. For the first question, students think about material covered over a span of chapters and classes. Students' summaries are more meaningful when they focus on content that is personally useful. For the second question, students think about what they don't know or what material is unclear to them. The leader will want to make sure this question is answered during the session. Here are other ways to assess students at the beginning of a session:

- **Ask questions.** Ask students what is giving them difficulties, what they did to prepare for the session, what problems they missed on the in-class quiz, and how long it took them to complete the homework assignment.

- **Give a quiz.** Either orally or on paper, students answer sample problems or summarize content.

- **Provide focus questions.** Written questions draw students' attention to the topics you expect to cover during a session and that they should understand by the end of the session. By answering these questions, students focus their attention on important content, predict ideas covered during the session, and realize what information they need to pay particular attention to. Chapters 1 and 2 open with focus questions.

ACTIVITY 4.2

ASSESSMENT EXAMPLE

Describe another way to assess students informally at the beginning of a session in your subject area.

MIDDLE OF SESSION

For maximum effectiveness, intersperse assessment throughout the session. Checking students' understanding periodically during a session is called *formative evaluation*. Formative evaluation usually happens at the close of one topic and before the start of another topic. Formative evaluation is important especially when covering complex and confusing information. This measurement need not be detailed or laborious and can occur when there is a natural break between topics or procedures. However, do make sure your assessment provides *meaningful, concrete evidence* of students' understanding. For example, in this text, activities are interspersed within chapters with the purpose of checking your (the reader's) understanding of subtopics.

Other examples of formative assessment are when students:

- Teach a topic, formula, or section of the material to other students.
- Complete another, similar problem independently.
- Provide additional examples.
- Paraphrase or summarize information in their own words.
- Draw conclusions independently.

- Correct previous errors.
- Complete a set of problems.

ACTIVITY 4.3

TRY IT OUT

Cross and Angelo's (1988) "Punctuated Lecture" and "Punctuated Text" (Figure 4.1) are useful as a means to review course content, as well as a method for assessing how students are listening to lectures and reading assignments. Students reflect upon, identify, and share concentration problems and study strategies. Students work on ways to make listening and reading more active and engaging, with the goal of improving their concentration, understanding, and retention of subject matter.

Before continuing with this chapter, complete the Punctuated Text assessment tool to assess your reading behaviors and gauge the effectiveness of your reading and study strategies. Answer these questions:

- How much were you concentrating in your reading thus far?
- Did you get distracted? If so, how did you get your attention back?
- What are you doing to help you understand *and* remember the information you are reading?
- What do you expect to come next in this chapter?
- How do you envision using this tool in your own sessions?

FIGURE 4.1 Assessment techniques

Punctuated Lecture
1. How much were you concentrating on the lecture? Did you get distracted? If so, how did you get your attention back?
2. What were you doing to help you understand and remember the information that you were hearing?
3. What do you expect to come next in the lecture?

Punctuated Text
1. How much were you concentrating on the reading? Did you get distracted? If so, how did you get your attention back?
2. What were you doing to help you understand and remember the information that you were reading?
3. What do you expect to come next in the reading?

Source: Cross, K. P., & Angelo, T. A. (1988). *Classroom assessment techniques. A handbook for faculty.* Ann Arbor, MI: National Center for Research on the Improvement of Postsecondary Teaching and Learning.

END OF SESSION

Termed *summative assessment*, end-of-session evaluations represent the body of ideas or problems covered during a session. Whereas formative evaluation refers to smaller parts and topics, summative assessment refers to the totality of information covered during the session. Again, focus on *solid evidence* that each student has gained knowledge or skills. The following illustrate summative assessment methods. Students:

- Answer focus questions such as those at the end of Chapters 1 and 2.
- Complete sample tests.
- Summarize key information.
- Follow through with directives, such as *show, explain, summarize,* and *demonstrate.*
- Create test questions for one another.
- Apply a concept correctly.
- Complete a procedure independently.

ACTIVITY 4.4

THINKING AND ASSESSING

Your assessment methods should reflect the level of thinking required of students in the course. To answer the questions, refer either to Figure 4.2 below or to Figure 3.2 (in Chapter 3, p. 38).

FIGURE 4.2 Bloom's cognitive categories and assessment methods

Bloom's categories	Informal assessment methods
Evaluation level	Judge the merits of sample essay answers based on criteria from the course material.
Synthesis level	Create a summary sheet linking key ideas from a group discussion and information from a textbook chapter.
Analysis level	Categorize assessment methods according to cognitive level.
Application level	Demonstrate how to use formative assessment in a peer-led session.
Comprehension level	Provide examples of summative evaluation.
Knowledge level	Define summative evaluation.

- What levels of thinking correspond to each of the examples listed for middle-of-session (p. 46–47) and end-of-session (p. 48) assessment?
- Figure 4.2 provides a sample informal assessment method that corresponds to each cognitive level. Add another informal assessment method for each level. Share your examples with classmates.

WHAT *IS* AND *IS NOT* ADEQUATE EVIDENCE OF LEARNING?

Assessing students' understanding of a topic, concept, or procedure requires proof of learning. Your method of assessment should result in evidence that is both tangible and meaningful, that is, connected to course content and requirements. All the examples of assessment techniques for the beginning, middle, and end of sessions will produce concrete evidence of learning.

Though frequently used, the following *do not* represent concrete evidence that students truly comprehend content:

Yes/no questions. For example: *Do you understand this? Is this clear? Do you have any problems? Do you have any questions about this?*

Students' positive comments. For example: *I understand it now. Oh, I see how to do that problem. Yes, the concept is clear to me.*

Students' facial expressions and body language. For example: *smiling, heads nodding, conveying confidence, expressions of relief, expressions indicating that "the light bulb" has come on.*

The above gestures and comments can be signs that students understand the material; however, they are not adequate and reliable indicators of learning. Do follow up with techniques that offer more solid proof regarding students' understanding, retention, and abilities to apply the information.

ACTIVITY 4.5

OBSERVATION

When observing fellow peer educators, make note of how they incorporate assessment within their sessions. Use these questions to guide your observations:

1. **Beginning of session:** Did the peer educator assess students' baseline knowledge, level of preparation, and/or use of learning strategies?

Continued

ACTIVITY 4.5 *Continued*

> - If yes, describe what the peer educator did.
> - What level or type of thinking was required of students?
> - Did the assessment result in tangible and meaningful evidence of students' learning? If yes, describe. If no, what would you recommend the peer educator change or do?
>
> 2. **During the session:** Did the peer educator assess students' understanding of particular topics, subsections, procedures, problems, formulas, and the like?
>
>   - If yes, describe what the peer educator did.
>   - What level or type of thinking was required of students?
>   - Did the assessment result in tangible and meaningful evidence of students' learning? If yes, describe. If no, what would you recommend the peer educator change or do?
>
> 3. **End of session:** Did the peer educator assess students' knowledge of information covered during the session?
>
>   - If yes, describe what the peer educator did.
>   - What level or type of thinking was required of students?
>   - Did the assessment result in tangible and meaningful evidence of students' learning? If yes, describe. If no, what would you recommend the peer educator change or do?

Closing

ACTIVITY 4.6

PRACTICE SUMMATIVE ASSESSMENT

For this activity, you need a blank index card and a partner (Gershwin, 1994).

1. On the front of the card, summarize the "clearest point" of the chapter. On the back, summarize the "muddiest point" of the chapter.

2. Explain your clearest point to your partner, and vice versa. Then, you each state your muddiest point and see if your partner can help clarify this point for you. Partners can ask one another questions about their clearest and muddiest points. (In a one-on-one tutoring situation, the student explains out loud to the peer educator.)

3. You and your partner report to others in the class or session about clearest and muddiest points.

   - See if others can clarify the muddiest points, or
   - Students are assigned muddiest points in order to find out explanations or answers for the next session, or
   - In a one-on-one tutorial setting, ask questions and talk through the student's clearest and muddiest points. Emphasize ways the student can better understand the information before the next session.

LEARNING STRATEGY: PREPARING FOR EXAMS

Students you work with may have little experience with how to adequately prepare for college-level exams. Before considering which test preparation strategies that you should promote in your sessions, assess how well you prepare for exams.

ACTIVITY 4.7

EXAM PREPARATION

First, evaluate how thoroughly you prepare for important tests by completing the checklist in Figure 4.3.

FIGURE 4.3 Checklist to assess exam preparation

When preparing for a major exam, do you . . .	Yes, most of the time	Sometimes	Rarely or never
1. Find out about the exam—material covered, type of questions, length and time constraints?			
2. Add extra study time 5–7 days before the exam?			
3. Utilize a study location free from distractions?			
4. Review lecture, text, and/or lab notes and identify main points to know for the exam?			
5. Develop a test review guide that summarizes and consolidates important information?			

Continued

ACTIVITY 4.7 *Continued*

FIGURE 4.3 *Continued*

6. Participate in available professor review sessions?			
7. Participate in available peer-led review sessions or study groups?			
8. Recite out loud as you study to increase retention?			
9. Practice sample problems and questions?			
10. Maintain adequate sleep, regular exercise, and healthy eating to sustain your energy, concentration, and retention?			

Second, summarize your answers to the ten questions. Overall, are you satisfied with how you prepare for tests? Why or why not? Identify and describe one strategy that is effective for you when preparing for an important exam. What makes this strategy so helpful for you?

Third, identify a strategy from the checklist that you want to utilize more. Develop and apply a personal goal regarding your use of this strategy when preparing for an upcoming test in a course. Adhere to the criteria for establishing goals, as outlined in Chapter 1:

1. Be specific.

2. Be realistic.

3. Have a time constraint.

4. Write it down.

5. Say it out loud.

6. Afterward, evaluate your success.

7. Share with another person.

Complete the goal statement: *When preparing for my exam in [subject/course], I will:*

After the exam, revisit your goal and assess the effectiveness of the strategy. Will you continue to use the strategy when preparing for your next test? Why or why not?

ACTIVITY 4.8

SUMMARIZING IMPORTANT INFORMATION

Summative evaluation methods can be effective tools for test preparation. Item #5 on the checklist (Figure 4.3, p. 51) refers to developing a test review guide to summarize and consolidate important information. Most often test review guides are in the form of an outline, study cards, idea map, or summary chart. However, methods for evaluating cumulative learning can serve also as tools for test preparation. For example, the summative assessment for Activity 4.6 on p. 50 can be used also for exam preparation.

Chain Notes (Cross & Angelo, 1988) is another summative assessment technique that can be used as a test review guide. Chain Notes are especially appropriate for small-group, course-based sessions; try it out with a group of peer educators in your training class.

1. At the top of a sheet of paper (or use a computer screen), write: *What is one thing you learned in the chapter that is important for you to know?*
2. One person answers the question and then passes the sheet to another classmate who adds a different answer.
3. Pass the sheet around until everyone has added different information.
4. Each student receives a copy of the completed Chain Note to use for a chapter review sheet.

Suggestions from Experienced Peer Educators

HOW DO YOU ASSESS STUDENTS' UNDERSTANDING?

In order to teach, one must know. Therefore, provide opportunities for students to teach one another. Give each group of students a relevant, yet complex topic related to the course. Each group develops a short, coherent presentation about that topic—similar to an oral answer to an essay question. As students work together to identify and organize content pertinent to their topic, they are actively thinking about and learning key information. During each presentation, urge the other students to ask questions. This method tests students' understanding of main concepts and prepares them for upcoming exams. (Becky B.)

At the beginning of a session, give a quiz consisting of 2–3 questions about content covered during the last session. At the end of the session, give one question that tests students' understanding of what they did. (Talia M.)

Start each session by discussing current material and asking questions. Students cannot use their notes. This method helps gauge which topics students are having problems with. (Shaun M.)

Make worksheets that represent a general overview of the material. These worksheets assess what students know or do not know, and highlight areas that should be focused on during the session. (Meg C.)

Use mini-quizzes throughout the session to assess how well students are retaining information. This technique lets students know what they need to focus on when studying. Also, students practice questions similar to those on the course exams. (Katie B.)

Develop a bank of problems for students to work on during sessions. Compile problems that represent a variety of types and difficulty levels. During your sessions, focus on those problems that fit students' abilities and interests. This creates flexible and efficient sessions. (Josh K.)

References

Cross, K. P., & Angelo, T. A. (1988). *Classroom assessment techniques. A handbook for faculty.* Ann Arbor, MI: National Center for Research on the Improvement of Postsecondary Teaching and Learning.

Gershwin, M. C. (1994, Winter). The mind-workout: Cooling your class down with interactive techniques. (p. 2). *Newsletter of the Skills for a Competitive Workforce Program.* Denver: Community College and Occupational Education System.

CHAPTER 5

Collaborative Learning and Group Work

OPENING: PREDICTING

Before reading the chapter, predict the answers to the following questions.

1. What is collaborative learning?
2. Why is collaborative learning an important aspect of academic support sessions?
3. How is collaborative learning implemented in peer-led sessions?
4. Describe a collaborative learning scenario.

Next, form a group of two to five classmates. Each shares his or her answers, with the goal of devising a group answer for each question. After completing the chapter, your group will have the opportunity to compare answers with other groups.

Nobody is as smart as everybody.

— Kevin Kelly, author

Collaborative Learning

At the postsecondary level, the lecture format is the most common manner by which information is presented in a class. As described in Chapter 2, this format is largely a passive approach toward learning because the instructor (the person who already knows the information) does most of the talking while the students (the people who are learning the information) sit and listen. To increase students' learning, academic support sessions should be in a format different from lecture, that is, a format that strengthens understanding and remembering of content. Collaborative learning is such a format. In a collaborative learning setting, the peer educator guides students to work collectively on a common task. Underpinning collaborative learning is the importance of shared experiences and contributions in the learning process (Casazza, 1998). By working together to master content, students will become more involved, responsible, and, eventually, independent in their learning. As theorist Lev Vygotsky (1978) stated, "What the [learner] is able to do in collaboration today, he will be able to do independently tomorrow."

Figure 5.1 summarizes key differences between the traditional lecture setting and a collaborative learning setting. In collaborative learning, students become resources of information and knowledge. They help one another to understand course content by asking and answering each other's questions, providing examples and explaining concepts, solving problems, and working together toward the common goal of learning course content.

FIGURE 5.1 Contrasting learning formats

Lecture format	Collaborative format	Examples
The instructor relays information to students, who assume a passive role.	Students communicate with each other and assume an active role.	
Learning involves individual, isolated effort.	Learning involves shared, team effort.	
Students primarily listen and take notes, allowing them to exert minimal attention and thought.	Within a group, students review content and solve problems, requiring them to concentrate and to think.	
Students tend to position themselves among peers who are familiar to them.	Conducive to heterogeneous groupings; promotes diverse relationships among students.	

ACTIVITY 5.1

EXAMPLES OF COLLABORATIVE LEARNING

When have you participated in a collaborative learning situation? In Figure 5.1, for each element associated with collaborative learning, provide a personal example of your experiences with collaborative learning. Your examples do not have to be classroom-based—consider other learning situations, such as summer camp experiences; a job, either paid or volunteer; an experience in church, Scouts, or other organization; or even an informal task, like cooking a meal. Share examples among class members.

COLLABORATIVE LEARNING GUIDELINES

What contributes to effective collaborative learning? How can you best get students to work together for a common objective? What is your role within a collaborative learning setting? The following "do's" and "don'ts" provide answers to these questions from the peer educator's viewpoint.

Do...

Publicize the benefits of collaborative work. (See the beginning-of-chapter quote.)

Plan ahead; think about how to best organize and structure each session. Careful preplanning produces the most successful collaborative settings. (See Activity 5.4, p. 63.)

Create a comfortable, cohesive, and trusting learning environment. Smile, have a friendly yet professional demeanor, sit among students, use students' names, have students introduce themselves to one another, and intersperse humor in sessions.

Set ground rules. Expect students to prepare for each session, complete homework, participate in the session, and turn off cell phones and electronic devices.

Assign activities that are meaningful and challenging. Center group work on tasks that require students to think about and apply course information. Include hands-on and experiential activities. Examples of appropriate collaborative activities are:

- Creating an outline or chart that summarizes class notes or readings.
- Tackling practice questions.
- Solving a set of problems.
- Developing examples.
- Creating models.
- Simulating case studies.
- Teaching the material to one another.
- Evaluating each other's essays.
- Predicting exam questions.
- Rehearsing a presentation.
- Playing games, which are particularly appropriate and popular for review before tests.

Encourage students to take risks. Praise students' attempts, allow for wrong answers, and model how to think through problems.

Assign and interchange individual roles and responsibilities within groups. Examples are:

- Leader—keeps the group on task.
- Recorder—keeps accurate answers and organizes notes.
- Time-keeper—ensures that the group is progressing at an appropriate pace.
- Presenter(s)—gives the group's final report, explains how the group solved the problem, demonstrates the activity, or summarizes the group's work.

Rotate among students, monitoring the group work: Are students focused on the topic? Do they have questions? Are members working together, with equal effort, and making steady progress?

Remain flexible. If one collaborative setup or activity is not working well, switch to another.

Don't...

- *Slow down for students who are not prepared or are not keeping up with their work and lagging behind.* Instead, work at maintaining an appropriate level, pace, and quality of content in sessions.
- *Let dominating students take over sessions.*
- *Let criticism and negativity permeate sessions.* If students become overly critical of instructors or course content, turn their attention to how they can adapt and be as successful as possible in that course and with that instructor.
- *Be rigid with plans.* The unexpected happens, so make adjustments as necessary.
- *Remain satisfied with the status quo.* Take risks; try out different activities, approaches, and group configurations (see next section). Critique yourself. Seek to improve sessions by soliciting students' assessments and suggestions.

GROUP CONFIGURATIONS

The following are ways to organize students and activities to enhance collaborative learning.

Course-based sessions. Because course-based sessions include those students enrolled in a targeted course section(s), there is a ready-made pool of students with common course content, requirements, and expectations. Course-based sessions naturally lend themselves to collaborative learning activities. The number of students attending any one course-based session often varies. Therefore, the peer educator needs to be prepared for dividing students into smaller group sizes to better accommodate the collaborative learning format. An ideal group size is three to five students, though group size can vary according to the activity and the total number students who attend the session.

Be aware that students tend to sit in the same location from session to session. Students often sit with classmates they are friends with or who become friends over time. Sitting in the same seats allows for a heightened comfort level as students get accustomed to the course and to your weekly sessions. However, over time, students working in the same groups can become stale or even problematic, such as when cliques form and new students feel ostracized. Do take it upon yourself to make changes—regroup students, rearrange furniture, and shift the focus—when needed to strengthen the collaborative learning environment. Here are several ways to make such changes:

- Count off students by groups as they enter the room.
- Write table or group numbers on the back of worksheets or sign-in sheets that students receive.
- Mix students of varying ability levels so that in each group the higher-achieving students can assist the lower-achieving students.
- Mix first-time students with seasoned participants.
- Activity stations: Create several (usually three to four) different activities. Place each at a different table or corner of the room. Divide students into groups corresponding to the number of activity stations. Each group of students rotates from station to station. To keep groups moving at the same pace, set up time limits for each activity.
- Group/regroup: First, subdivide a larger topic or chapter into sections. Assign each group a different subtopic, section, or set of problems to know thoroughly enough to teach others. Then, reassign students into new groups so that each group has a student who knows each topic. In each group, one student teaches the others, rotating so that all have the time to teach their topics. For example, create three groups, each with three members and a common topic to learn: Group 1: topic A, Group 2: topic B, Group 3: topic C. Then, reconfigure three new groups so that each group contains a student who knows topic A, a student who knows topic B, and a student who knows topic C.

Walk-in tutoring. Planning for walk-in sessions can be challenging, especially if students from differing course levels (such as any 100-level mathematics course) or instructors (such as any section of intermediate Spanish) are eligible to attend your sessions. Consider the following methods for grouping students for collaborative learning.

- Group students together who are in the same section, have the same instructor, or are in the same course level.
- Group students together who are experiencing similar problem areas or are focused on similar topics.
- Place a student who has mastered a topic with others who have questions. The proficient student can assist the others, at least until you are able to attend to the group.

Pre-exam sessions. For both course-based and walk-in tutorial sessions, students' attendance often surges immediately preceding a test. Arranging students into smaller groups makes these extra-large sessions not only more manageable but also more effective. Do set up activities in which clusters of students teach and support one another.

In addition, consider publicizing attendance restrictions for pre-exam review sessions. For instance, from the start of the semester, let students know that, in order to attend a session immediately preceding a major exam, they need to attend a specified number of sessions between exams. Be sure to communicate the twofold purpose of the restrictions:

1. To reduce the number of students who try to cram right before an exam and are misusing academic support services.

2. Encourage students to attend sessions *regularly* to maximize the benefits of collaborative learning and, ultimately, earn higher grades.

ACTIVITY 5.2

OBSERVING

Observe another peer educator's collaborative learning session. Use the "do" and "don't" guidelines on pages 57–58 to critique the session. Look at the strong aspects, as well as areas for improvement.

DEALING WITH COMMON PROBLEMS

In an ideal world, students attend your academic support sessions prepared, motivated, in agreeable moods, and eager to work together. However, it is more realistic to expect that students attend with differing levels of preparation, achievement, motivation, and involvement. Sometimes students disagree, socialize too much, or have negative attitudes. These and similar situations can disrupt a collaborative learning format, throwing off even your best-laid plans. In sessions, it is your responsibility to monitor students' activities, involvement, and behaviors. What should you do when encountering student behaviors and attitudes that spoil your sessions? Activity 5.3 addresses how you can respond to common problem situations.

ACTIVITY 5.3

RESPONDING TO PROBLEMS

Figure 5.2 lists five common situations that disrupt collaborative learning, with room for you to add two possible solutions for each situation. Work in pairs or small groups to describe ways to resolve each problem. If possible, ask experienced peer educators for their recommendations. Share your answers with others in your training class.

FIGURE 5.2 Common problems

Situation 1: One student dominates the group, not allowing others to contribute. This becomes demoralizing for other students who want to contribute.
Solutions:

1.

2.

Situation 2: Tension between two students disrupts the mutual learning and sense of community that you want to develop among students.
Solutions:

1.

2.

Situation 3: Students are coming to sessions increasingly less prepared. As a result, you have been giving them information, explanation, and answers. Students now expect that at each session you will provide them with important course material.
Solutions:

1.

2.

Situation 4: Two new students start attending your group sessions. To answer the many questions that they ask, you backtrack and reiterate information covered previously. This slows the pace of each session. Students who were attending regularly are becoming frustrated to the point that some of them have stopped coming.
Solutions:

1.

2.

Situation 5: One student continually comes 15 to 20 minutes late. She always sits next to her friend in the back of the room and begins a conversation, which is distracting to nearby students (who give her disapproving glares). You stopped her after the last session and politely asked her to arrive on time. She agreed; however, today she again arrived late. You don't want to be mean to another student and are at a loss what to do.
Solutions:

1.

2.

PLANNING SESSIONS

Successful collaborative learning requires careful preplanning. Figure 5.3 contains two separate plans for 50-minute sessions, using the following outline:

- **Topic**: Identify a specific topic that is important yet difficult for students. Think about what students likely will need to know about this topic.

- **Objective**: Consider how students can best learn the information. What do you want students to accomplish within the session?

- **Opening** (approximately 5–10 minutes): Plan an activity that will focus students' attention and launch the session. How will you introduce the topic to students?

- **Main body** (approximately 25–40 minutes): This segment contains the major activities. Aim for collaborative experiences that are structured, relevant, and engaging. Provide an array of approaches for students to understand, organize, and recall the targeted information.

- **Closing** (approximately 5–20 minutes): Choose activities that will bring closure to the session, such as a final assessment, review of key information, sharing of results, ensuring correct answers, answering questions, checking for concerns, reflecting on progress, or previewing upcoming topics/sessions. Will you have concrete evidence whether students have or have not accomplished your original objective?

- **Reflections**: Afterward, while the session is still fresh in your mind, summarize briefly your impressions of the activities and interactions. Think about what went particularly well and should be repeated. Also, what activity or event was not successful, and why? Jot down notes about a student, a topic for follow-up, an idea for the next session, or other things to remember when planning for future sessions. Also, what progress have you noted from one session to the next?

These written reflections will enhance the continuity of your sessions. Moreover, by critiquing each session, you become cognizant of your strengths, your weaknesses, and your overall growth in the peer educator role.

FIGURE 5.3 Sample session plans

<u>**Topic**</u>: DNA

<u>**Objective**</u>: Students understand correct steps for transcription and translation.

<u>**Segments**</u>

I. Opening: Review by having each student say one piece of information that we covered last week. (5 min.)

II. Main body: Divide students into four groups. Rotating around four stations, each group works on a poster board in which they put pieces in the correct steps for DNA transcription and translation. (25 min.)

III. Closing: Give students time to copy the completed transcription/translation in their notes and ask questions. Then, give them a short pop quiz to test their understanding of the topic. (20 min.)

Reflections

- Opening activity was useful way to get students prepped for the session. At first, students gave me blank stares; then they looked back at their notes; finally each recited a different topic.

- Because only six students attended, I divided them into two groups. The work stations took much longer than anticipated—used 3/4 stations, saving other one for the next session.

- Did not have time for pop quiz; will probably use the questions as an opening for Thurs. session.

- Rachel (one of my regulars) has not attended recently; I will send an email message to check on her.

Topic: Immune response

Objective: To understand 1) immune response, 2) similarities and differences of t-dependent and t-independent antigens.

Segments

I. Opening: As students enter room, they receive a worksheet with a number indicating which table they sit at. Then, I give them directions. (5 min.)

II. Main body: Each group has different items to complete and put on the board. (15 min.) Each group explains its work to the other students. (10 min.) Students role-play the "skit" on t-dependent and t-independent antigens and act out the immune response. (15 min.)

III. Closing: A student explains immune response to other students who ask questions. (5 min.)

Reflections: Prior to this session, students worked in the same groups and resisted my suggestion to change seats. Passing out worksheets with different table numbers made the students sit with other people. I started by having students introduce themselves to others at their table. I was hesitant about this opening activity, but the new groupings went smoothly. Students even role-played willingly for the skit. Next time, in addition to writing a table number, I will write a group role (leader, recorder, monitor, etc.) so that people participate with differing responsibilities. Overall, I realize how much students benefit from a mixture of activities and people (even though I might have to initiate the changes!).

ACTIVITY 5.4

PLAN A SESSION

For your subject area, develop a session plan that incorporates collaborative learning and group work.

1. Decide on a topic and corresponding learning objective(s).

2. Choose appropriate activities for the three session segments—opening, main body, and closing.

3. Share your plan with others in your class; seek their suggestions for ways to change or improve your session plan. Your instructor might ask you to simulate a group session by trying out your plans with one another.

Closing

LEARNING STRATEGY: GRAPHIC ORGANIZERS

College students often feel overwhelmed about how to effectively and efficiently read and study large amounts of complex material. Furthermore, many students struggle with how to combine important ideas in print with key topics covered in class. A relevant collaborative activity is developing graphic organizers, which are visual summaries of information in a variety of formats: concept maps or webs, charts, graphs, timelines, flow charts, and the like. Graphic organizers help students synthesize, categorize, and organize information obtained from assigned readings, class notes, and online sources.

Figure 5.4 contains examples of graphic organizers that peer educators used in their sessions. The common goal was to create a visual summary of the main ideas, important supporting ideas, and relationships among these ideas. In each case, the peer educator provided the overall framework or structure. Then, in groups, students collaborated to fill in the guide completely, correctly, and concisely. As the semester progressed, peer educators expected students to take increasing responsibility, with an end goal that students independently would develop graphic organizers to use for review and study before quizzes and tests.

FIGURE 5.4 Sample graphic organizers

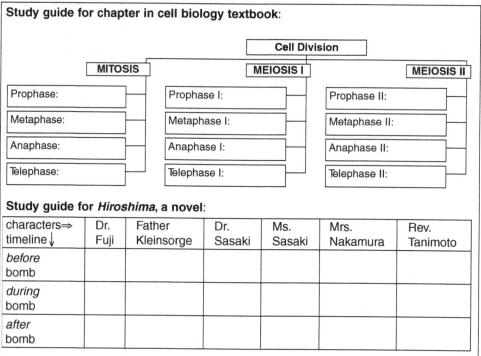

Study guide for chapter in cell biology textbook:

Cell Division — MITOSIS, MEIOSIS I, MEIOSIS II

MITOSIS	MEIOSIS I	MEIOSIS II
Prophase:	Prophase I:	Prophase II:
Metaphase:	Metaphase I:	Metaphase II:
Anaphase:	Anaphase I:	Anaphase II:
Telephase:	Telephase I:	Telephase II:

Study guide for *Hiroshima*, a novel:

characters⇒ timeline↓	Dr. Fuji	Father Kleinsorge	Dr. Sasaki	Ms. Sasaki	Mrs. Nakamura	Rev. Tanimoto
before bomb						
during bomb						
after bomb						

Study guide for a unit on *Protest Movements of the 1960s*, combining text information, articles, and class notes:

1960s Movements:	Civil Rights Movement *(Later Phase)*	Women's Rights Movement *(Early Phase)*	Vietnam War Protest Movement	American Indian Movement
Important People				
Important Terms/Ideas				
Significance				
Suggestions for Learning				

ACTIVITY 5.5

COLLABORATIVE GRAPHIC ORGANIZER

This is an activity for three to five people. Complete steps 1 and 2 individually; then, complete steps 3 and 4 as a group.

1. Describe three strategies that you use to help you learn important information from *reading assignments*.

2. Describe three strategies that you use to help you learn important information from *class notes*.

3. In your group, each person shares his or her list of six strategies. Then, create a graphic organizer (use any format) summarizing the learning strategies used by the collective group.

4. If there are other groups doing this activity, share completed graphic organizers with each other. Answer these questions: What were the dynamics of the group? Who took charge orchestrating this activity? Did all participate equally? Explain. How would you change this activity? Present an example of how you could use graphic organizers in your peer-led sessions.

CHECK FOR UNDERSTANDING

At the beginning of the chapter, your group predicted answers to four focus questions:

1. What is collaborative learning?
2. Why is collaborative learning an important aspect of academic support sessions?
3. How is collaborative learning implemented in peer-led sessions?
4. Describe a collaborative learning scenario.

Return to your original group. Exchange answers with another group. Then, each group:

- Decides on answers to each of the four questions. What information should be included to answer sufficiently each of the four questions? Because you will be checking another group's answers, what criteria will you use to evaluate correct, complete, and clear answers?
- Critique the other group's answers. For each answer, assign a letter grade and write an explanation for why you assigned that grade.
- Return answers so that each group can read what the others have written.

Suggestions from Experienced Peer Educators

HOW DO YOU CREATE COLLABORATION AMONG STUDENTS?

To facilitate discussion, I direct students to work in pairs for the first part of a session. Then, we move into a forum of open discussion. This setup seems to increase both interaction and learning. I often notice a light bulb going on above their heads; I see that they really understand the material. (Troy P.)

Group students together who are working on the same subject. Then, as a group, students work on answering each other's questions. If someone knows what to do, he or she explains it to the others while I help a different group. If the explanation was not enough, then I will add information. (Nicole M.)

Students work best if they trust the leader, feel comfortable with others in their group, and expect everyone to participate. (Kia T.)

Make the session a discussion rather than a question-and-answer review. When a student has a question, let others answer it. If nobody knows the answer, keep asking questions until someone can. (Kyle T.)

 Tell students you are unsure of the answer. This motivates students to work among themselves to figure out answers. (Malika V.)

References

Casazza, M. E. (1998). Strengthening practice with theory. *Journal of Developmental Education, 22*(2), 14–20, 43.

Vygotsky, L. S. (1978). *Mind in society*. Cambridge, MA: Harvard University Press.

CHAPTER 6

Tutoring as a Proactive Process

OPENING: HIGHLIGHTING AND ANNOTATING

Highlighting can be a useful learning and study tool for reading assignments, as well as for review of lecture notes. Highlighting involves decision making as to what ideas are and are not important and, when done effectively, aids understanding and retention of important content.

If you give a man a fish, he will eat it and soon be hungry. If you teach a man to fish, he will never be hungry.

— Chinese proverb

ACTIVITY 6.1

GUIDELINES

Highlighting is most effective when applied accordingly:

1. First, read a section. Then, go back and highlight important terms and ideas (as opposed to highlighting as you read). *Explain why this is recommended.*

2. Highlight words and phrases, as opposed to whole sentences or entire paragraphs. *Explain why this is recommended.*

3. Add annotations, or markings, that help to summarize, clarify, organize, emphasize, and personalize key content. Combining annotations with highlighting expands the thought process, creating a more valuable learning and study aid. "Markings combined with highlighting or underlining is an effective study guide because you are *interacting* with the text material, making ideas as explicit as possible" (Lipsky, 2008, p. 83). Examples of markings in text pages are:

- Marginal notes that summarize a long passage, provide examples of a concept, or clarify why a topic is important.
- References to in-class material.
- Numbers that emphasize order of ideas.
- Symbols that accentuate importance or connections of ideas (? * →).

Provide other examples of annotations or markings that you use in readings and notes.

ACTIVITY 6.2

APPLYING

As you read this chapter, create a highlighting-plus-annotations study guide. At the conclusion of the chapter, you will be directed to share and critique study guides created by members of your training class.

Introduction

This chapter addresses a process that maximizes student learning in a one-on-one tutoring session. In such a setting, you have the opportunity to be more proactive in guiding—and at times pushing—the student toward developing an effective and efficient system for learning and studying college-level content.

A Proactive Model

Generally speaking, course-based models of peer assistance, such as Peer-Led Team Learning and Supplemental Instruction, produce stronger learning outcomes than does traditional tutoring (Arendale, 2004). One reason for the disparity in outcomes is that content of course-based sessions is linked to a targeted course. This linkage results in higher final grades and persistence rates for participating students. Another reason for the differences in learning outcomes is that often college students associate the term "tutoring" with remediation or failure. As a result, students avoid seeking help until they face academic difficulty or are panicked just before an exam. Students' sporadic attendance at tutoring counters the goal of effective peer assistance.

Creating linkages with targeted courses is one way that tutoring programs can strengthen student learning. As the tutor, reach out to the instructor and the students. The more the content of your session is linked with course requirements and instructor expectations, the more relevant the session will be for the student. Whenever possible, attend class sessions for the subject. You will obtain a clearer vision of how the instructor teaches, how students respond, as well as specific content and pace for the course. Also, when students see you in class, they are more likely to seek tutorial assistance early and recurrently, *before* they experience significant problems. Furthermore, communicate with the instructor regularly. Ask about particular problem areas that you might emphasize in your sessions. Inquire if the instructor has supplemental materials or practice problems that can be useful in your tutoring sessions.

ACTIVITY 6.3

REFLECTION

1. Do you agree that the term "tutoring" connotes remediation or failure? Why or why not? What other terms might you substitute for tutor or tutoring?

2. What are the advantages of tutoring? List two advantages of one-on-one tutoring over course-based programs.

3. A proactive model of tutoring incorporates universal components of effective peer-led sessions. Describe two to three components that you should be mindful to incorporate into your tutoring sessions. (Do revisit previous chapters to help you answer this question.)

The Tutoring Cycle

A factor in college students' development as responsible, independent learners is recognition that learning is a continual process. Likewise, implement tutoring as an ongoing process, as illustrated in Figure 6.1. As you read about these interrelated steps, be aware that they are not always distinct and neatly separate. At times, the steps overlap one another or are skipped completely.

FIGURE 6.1 Cyclical steps for tutoring

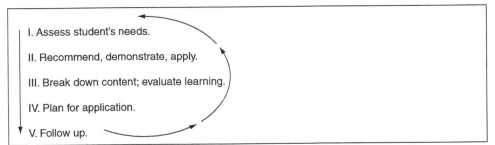

I. Assess student's needs.

II. Recommend, demonstrate, apply.

III. Break down content; evaluate learning.

IV. Plan for application.

V. Follow up.

STEP I. ASSESS THE STUDENT'S NEEDS

At the beginning of a session, determine a baseline as to what the student does and does not know. Become aware of the student's strengths—what the student understands and can do independently—as well as the student's weaknesses and gaps in knowledge. Seek to capitalize on the student's strengths as you work on building both understanding of content and application of learning strategies. This first step helps to set an overall direction for what to accomplish during the session.

Figure 6.2 illustrates a general continuum of knowledge and skills. The top of the continuum represents mastery of particular content, as evidenced by a person's ability to evaluate, synthesize, analyze, and/or apply independently. The bottom of the continuum indicates that the person has no knowledge or understanding of the particular topic or skill. Focusing on content that a student has already mastered would be an inefficient use of a session—the student would become bored and restless and likely would not return. On the other hand, working on a topic for which the student has no knowledge also is an inefficient use of time, leading to frustration for both the student and you.

A challenge is for you to find a level for which the student has some knowledge of the content but cannot understand, apply, or analyze independently (Vygotsky, 1978). It is at this level that you likely will provide the greatest help—and reap the greatest rewards—in your work with a student. By reinforcing key concepts, clarifying steps, introducing additional problems, providing more practice, rehearsing questions, and the like, you will be helping the student build a higher level of understanding or even mastery of the content.

FIGURE 6.2 Levels of understanding

Mastery of content and skills—has a full understanding and can apply independently.

↑

↑

Has acquired some understanding but cannot apply independently.

↑

↑

Has no knowledge and is fully dependent upon others for content.

ACTIVITY 6.4

ASSESSING A STUDENT'S NEEDS

How does a tutor gauge an appropriate starting point? What are differing methods for assessing a student's knowledge level regarding content, as well as study techniques, attitude, and learning style? Brainstorm with others to identify at least four ways to assess a student's needs in order to establish the direction of a tutorial session. (For help with this activity, review Chapter 4.)

STEP II. RECOMMEND, DEMONSTRATE, AND APPLY

The more that you link content *and* strategies directly with the student's coursework, the more effective your session will be for the student. Thus, do integrate active learning strategies into each session. Do not assume that the student knows strategies for learning content, including basic techniques for managing time, being organized, taking notes, reading textbooks, and preparing for and taking exams. Whenever you recommend a specific learning strategy, be sure to demonstrate the strategy and then provide practice and reinforcement in the session, before the student tries it out during the week.

ACTIVITY 6.5

TRY IT OUT

With a partner, practice Steps I and II using the scenarios that follow. One person can role-play as the tutor while the other is the student; then, switch roles. Ask another classmate to watch and offer feedback about how effectively the tutor assesses, recommends, demonstrates, and has the student apply appropriate learning strategies.

1. The student is having problems with basic concepts in the text. The tutor finds out that the student is not reading the textbook.
2. The student is unprepared for the session. The student does not bring the textbook and lecture notes and has not done the assigned homework problems.
3. The student is struggling with content presented in class. The tutor notices that the student prints out copies of the PowerPoint notes before class but does not write on the notes during class. The student admits to having a difficult time paying attention to the instructor during class.
4. The student is feeling quite anxious about next week's midterm exam. The student is overwhelmed by how to prepare for this major test.

STEP III. BREAK DOWN CONTENT; EVALUATE LEARNING

To maximize a student's learning of complex and difficult content, *focus on one chunk of information* (or section of a topic, or step of a problem) *at a time*. Employ the following strategies as you work with a student toward understanding content:

Elicit information from the student. Ask questions about the material, guiding and prompting the student, as necessary (as opposed to just giving the student answers).

Relate information to real situations. Give examples and applications of topics. Model ways to figure out solutions and use information.

Provide adequate time-on-task for the student to practice and reflect.

Provide regular feedback.

Assess learning. Include concrete means to check the student's level of understanding before moving on to another topic, section, or problem.

Be supportive. View the student–tutor relationship as a learning partnership.

Encourage the student to take risks—to try problems, answer questions, use strategies, ask the instructor, and utilize other resources.

ACTIVITY 6.6

TUTORING STRATEGIES

What other strategies should you employ to maximize a student's learning of complex and difficult content? Starting with "focus on one chunk of information at a time," eight strategies are listed in the preceding section. Describe one additional strategy. A quick review of Chapters 3 and 4 will help you answer this question.

STEP IV. PLAN FOR APPLICATION

At the end of each tutoring session, work with the student to develop a plan of application. The purpose of this plan is to get a commitment from the student to continue work on specific content, as well as to apply strategies, assess accomplishments, and return for a follow-up session. This plan need not be elaborate or tedious. Figure 6.3 illustrates an informal plan directing the student to summarize what was covered during a tutoring session and what to work on outside of the session. Remember: a student is more likely to continue practice and transfer of strategies outside of sessions if the student completes a written plan.

FIGURE 6.3 Sample summary of tutoring session

Date/time _____ Student name _____

Tutor _____ Subject _____

The purpose of this session summary is for you and your tutor to keep track of your progress throughout the semester, including the content you are covering and the strategies you are using. At the end of each session, respond to the following four statements. *Be precise.* Then, give it to your tutor to read and offer revisions before signing.

1. Describe what you worked on and accomplished during this session.

2. Identify what you intend to work on before your next session.

3. Describe a specific learning or study strategy that you will implement this week.

4. Identify your next session:
    Tutor signature _____

Following is an example of thoughtful and appropriate student responses for statements 1–3 on the sample summary sheet. Note that the student targeted topics and provided brief explanations or information about the topics. Also, the student identified a specific and useful strategy for statement 3.

1. Describe what you worked on and accomplished during this session: *We worked on endochondral growth and intramembraneous growth, and made a chart summarizing characteristics of both. We discussed how humans grow and why we grow the way we do.*

2. Identify what you intend to work on before your next session: *The next section is about muscles—origin and insertion, synergists and antagonists.*

3. Describe a specific learning or study strategy that you will implement this week: *I will make summary charts. They really help by breaking topics down, making them easier to understand.*

The next example is a weak summary of a tutoring session. The student wrote quick, cursory answers, which are common for students who are new to tutoring and are unfamiliar with expectations of tutoring and the process of monitoring one's learning. Importantly, before signing the summary sheet, the tutor commented on how to strengthen the responses and then asked the student to make revisions.

Student's answers with tutor's comments:

1. Describe what you worked on and accomplished during this session: *We worked on the assignment due Friday because I got stuck.*

2. Identify what you intend to work on before your next session: *Try to read the book better.*

3. Describe a specific learning or study strategy that you will implement this week: *Going over the vocabulary.*

   Tutor comments: Provide more specific answers. For #1, explain what exactly you had problems with and what we did in the session to help you overcome these problems. For #2, be precise regarding the steps you *will do* (not just *try* to do!) to improve your reading of the text. For #3, what does "going over" mean? Provide more detail. Of the strategies we went over together, which one(s) will you be implementing this week?

Student's revision:

1. Describe what you worked on and accomplished during this session: *Since I couldn't do the worksheet on accrual and non-accrual, we went over what each means, what are the differences, and examples of how each is used.*

2. Identify what you intend to work on before your next session: *Complete the assignment due Friday. Also, begin reading the next chapter earlier in the week, either Mon. or Tues., and earlier in the day. Spread out reading over 3–4 days. Break up the chapter so that I read a section and answer the study guide questions before moving on to the next section.*

3. Describe a specific learning or study strategy that you will implement this week: *I will buy index cards. As I read each section, I will make a card for each of the boldfaced terms. The front will have the word, the back a short definition and original sentence. I then can use these cards to review important vocabulary over and over again.*

ACTIVITY 6.7

EVALUATE STUDENT RESPONSES

Assess the student's responses for each of the following session summary sheets. Write your evaluative comments and suggestions beside "Tutor comments." Then, share your comments with others in your training class.

1. Describe what you worked on and accomplished during this session: *I worked on correlations. Kelly [the tutor] explained it to me in a more in-depth way so I could understand it a lot better.*

2. Identify what you intend to work on before your next session: *I am going to write more examples and have questions ready to ask Kelly when I come back.*

3. Describe a specific learning or study strategy that you will implement this week: *I am going to write questions on my notes so I know that I know it!*

Tutor comments:

Continued

ACTIVITY 6.7 *Continued*

1. Describe what you worked on and accomplished during this session: *We reviewed the Arrherius Equation and unit assignment.*

2. Identify what you intend to work on before your next session: *Review material for exam, especially memorizing equations.*

3. Describe a specific learning or study strategy that you will implement this week: *Reteaching and repetition.*

Tutor comments:

1. Describe what you worked on and accomplished during this session: *Review for upcoming exam.*

2. Identify what you intend to work on before your next session: *Practice problems from quiz.*

3. Describe a specific learning or study strategy that you will implement this week: *Try to study a little bit each night and read the chapter.*

Tutor comments:

STEP V. FOLLOW UP

An incentive for a student to follow through with each plan of application is the knowledge that the tutor *will be* asking questions and tracking the student's progress. The plan of application from the previous session becomes the starting point for the next tutorial session. At this point, you begin the tutoring cycle anew by assessing the student's accomplishments. Based on the written plan or session summary, ask the student questions about what happened between sessions, including how well the student is understanding content and applying strategies. Then, continue with the subsequent steps.

Thus, the cyclical nature of tutoring builds on the student's previous work and progresses from session to session. You, the tutor, show the student how to break down information, figure out problems, provide personal examples, apply strategies, make content relevant, and utilize a range of active learning strategies. As the student experiences increasing success with course work, he or she realizes the value of participating in tutoring on an ongoing basis. Furthermore, over a period of time, you provide decreasing amounts of structure so that the student assumes more responsibility for course work and learning. The bottom line: by utilizing the tutorial cycle, you help students become more knowledgeable, confident, independent, and empowered college students.

ACTIVITY 6.8

TUTORING CYCLE: OBSERVING AND PRACTICING

1. Observe a tutorial session. Use the form provided in Figure 6.4 to evaluate the session.

FIGURE 6.4 Observation form for tutoring session

Use the following key to answer items 1–18:

Y—yes, clearly observed; **S**—somewhat observed;
N—not observed; **n/a**—not applicable.

1. Arrives on time and stays on schedule. _____

2. Is friendly and welcoming. _____

3. Follows up from previous session. _____

4. Makes frequent eye contact with the student. Uses the student's name. Smiles. _____

5. Creates an environment that is comfortable, supportive, yet oriented toward academics. _____

6. Assesses the needs of the student. _____

7. Paces activities during the session effectively. Stays involved during the session. _____

8. Uses open-ended, higher-level questions to stimulate thinking and learning. _____

9. Gives clues and directions that guide the student toward answers (instead of directly answering or giving information). _____

10. Is knowledgeable in the subject area. _____

11. Uses effective examples to clarify points. _____

12. Recommends, demonstrates, and practices approaches for learning content. Integrates learning strategies with content material. _____

13. Checks the student's understanding of content periodically. _____

14. Provides feedback regularly. _____

15. Adjusts the direction and pacing in response to the student's questions and needs. _____

16. Includes a plan of application for the student. Provides appropriate guidance and suggestions regarding completion of the plan. _____

17. Gets commitment from the student to return. _____

18. Ends the session on a positive note. _____

19. What are the exceptional parts of this session?

20. What suggestions do you have to improve the session?

Continued

ACTIVITY 6.8 *Continued*

> 2. To practice the tutoring cycle, devise role-playing scenarios with class-mates. One person replicates the role of a student with an academic problem, another person is the tutor, and the remaining people observe and then provide feedback regarding the simulated session. If you are working currently as a tutor, ask another person to complete a structured observation of your session, using the form in Figure 6.4.

Active Listening

A ctive listening involves attention, energy, and thought. The goal of active listening is to understand and remember important information. During class time, students should listen actively to decide which aspects of the lecture or presentation are important to know—that is, which topics they likely will need for a test, discussion, paper, or other assignment.

Active listening is especially important in a one-on-one tutorial session. From the start, a peer educator needs to analyze information given by the student and make an immediate decision about how to proceed in the session. Thus, decision making is an important component of active listening.

ACTIVITY 6.9

REFLECTING

In a written paragraph, compose your answer to the following questions. If you are part of a training class, compare and contrast the answers of your class-mates. Make revisions, as necessary, so that your class develops one final answer that is both practical and comprehensive. *In your role as peer educator, what important information do you need to understand and remember when listening to a student? What are you going to do with this information?*

ACTIVITY 6.10

ACTIVE LISTENING STRATEGIES

What strategies do you employ that help you listen actively in a class session? From the list of strategies in Figure 6.5, indicate which strategies you use on a regular basis. Next, decide which listening strategies are appropriate to use in your peer educator role, and write a brief explanation in the last column.

FIGURE 6.5 Active listening strategies

Active listening strategies	Do you use it as a student?	Should you use it as a peer educator? Explain.
1. Beforehand, review notes from the previous session.		
2. Have supplies ready to use—paper, pen, laptop, text, and other appropriate materials.		
3. Position yourself to see and hear clearly.		
4. Pay attention; be mindful of key ideas.		
5. Take notes, either written or on a computer.		
6. Be alert to verbal and nonverbal cues.		
7. Participate—ask and answer questions.		
8. Review your notes *soon* after the session, while the content is fresh in your mind.		
9. Do something with your notes, such as: • Organize pages. • Highlight important ideas. • Add explanations. • Add information from text or other readings. • Rewrite to make clearer. • Summarize key points.		
10. Follow up with resources, if appropriate. For example: • Seek additional information from instructor. • Go to tutoring or study/review sessions. • Use supplemental and online course materials.		

Listening cues. As a peer educator, you indicate to the students with whom you are working whether you are listening attentively to what they say. In Figure 6.5, strategy #6 refers to "verbal and nonverbal cues," which signal the importance of a piece of information. These cues also provide signals as to how attentive and responsive a person is to what you say. Imagine one-on-one conversations that you have with friends or family members. What clues does the other person give to indicate he or she is listening and understanding what you are saying? Think about what the other person articulates (verbal cues) and how the person acts (nonverbal cues) to communicate he or she is paying attention to what you are saying.

ACTIVITY 6.11

VERBAL AND NONVERBAL CUES

Figure 6.6 contains examples of verbal and a nonverbal cues that signal alertness and attentiveness of the listener. Provide additional examples. Be mindful of cues in your own conversations, and see if you can add at least four more verbal and nonverbal cues. Share with others in your training class.

FIGURE 6.6 Listening cues

Nonverbal cues	Verbal cues
Listener nods head.	Listener paraphrases the speaker.

Verbal Communication

In a peer educator role, there are many situations in which you need to express yourself verbally. You will be explaining steps, simplifying concepts, describing examples, suggesting strategies, and providing a variety of directives. In these and similar situations, you want to communicate effectively so that your message is understood clearly by students. Before reading about guidelines for communicating verbally, complete the following activity that focuses on providing clear, unambiguous instructions.

ACTIVITY 6.12

PRACTICE VERBAL COMMUNICATION

For this role-playing exercise, you play the tutor; find another person to be the student.

DIRECTIONS

1. Give the student a blank sheet of paper and a pencil with an eraser.
2. Tell the student that the objective of this activity is for the tutor to explain to the student how to draw an image, with this major stipulation: The student cannot see the image that the tutor is talking about, and the tutor cannot see what the student is drawing. Therefore, arrange your positions by sitting far enough apart, or back to back, or place something between you to block your views of each other's actions.
3. The tutor chooses one of the images in Figure 6.7.
4. The tutor begins giving directions to the student about how to replicate this image.
5. Both the tutor and student can talk and ask questions.
6. Stop when either of you is satisfied that the task is completed, or when either of you reaches a point of frustration.

FIGURE 6.7 Images for Activity 6.12

Image #1

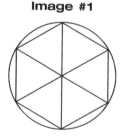

Image #2

Image #3: The tutor cannot say the word "house" when giving directions for this image.

Continued

7. Compare and contrast the real image with the image the student drew. How exact was the student's replication?

8. Discuss what contributed to the results. Consider what the tutor said, as well as the tone and inflection of the tutor's voice. As the tutor, how effectively were you able to communicate using only verbal directions?

GUIDELINES FOR VERBAL COMMUNICATION

The following principles will help you provide effective directions and explanations to students. As you read them, place a check next to the ones you applied in Activity 6.12, when you gave directions to the student.

__ **Provide a purpose, overview, or ending point**. Students will better understand the subtopics, steps, or parts of the material if you first provide the overall picture or objective of the activity.

__ **Be precise**. "Move your pencil several inches" is not as useful as "move your pencil 2 inches."

__ **Proceed one step at a time**. Check for understanding after each step, such as "Explain what you are going to do next." Be prepared to repeat the step or to paraphrase information, if necessary.

__ **Seek feedback from the student**. For example: "Describe what the image looks like now." "Tell me what is unclear to you." Listen to the student's answer and respond accordingly.

__ **Encourage give and take between tutor and student**. You want the student to be comfortable enough to ask questions and try out possibilities.

__ **Be patient**. Give the student time to think and to do. Remember, what comes easily for you does not necessarily come easily for the student.

__ **Express your limits**. Know when to say "I don't know" or "Maybe another tutor can provide a better explanation for you" or "You should see your instructor."

What other principles can you add to this list?

ACTIVITY 6.13

ACTIVE LISTENING AND VERBAL COMMUNICATION

Go back to your observations and practice of tutoring sessions in Activity 6.8. (p. 77). Refer to Figure 6.5 (p. 79) and the preceding section, "Guidelines for Verbal Communication." What listening and verbalizing strategies did you observe? Practice these strategies when simulating peer-led sessions, both in groups and one-on-one. Role-playing scenarios for practice are in the Instructor's Manual.

Closing

ACTIVITY 6.14

FOLLOW UP—HIGHLIGHTING AND ANNOTATING

1. Exchange study guides with other members of your training class. As you review others' study guides, consider what revisions, if any, you should make on your highlighting and annotations.

2. Answer these evaluative questions:

   • How would you use your highlighting-plus-annotating study guide when preparing for a quiz or test?

   • Did you implement the two highlighting guidelines described at the beginning of this chapter (read first, then highlight; highlight words and phrases)? If no, explain your reason. If yes, explain whether the strategies helped you to read and understand chapter content.

   • How can you use this learning strategy in your peer-led sessions?

References

Arendale, D. (1997). Supplemental Instruction (SI): Review of research concerning the effectiveness of SI from the University of Missouri-Kansas City and other institutions from across the United States. In S. Mioduski & G. Enright (Eds.). *Proceeding of the 17th and 18th annual institutes for learning assistance professionals: 1996 and 1997* (pp. 1–25). Tucson, AZ: University Learning Center, University of Arizona. Retrieved November 25, 2008, from http://www.pvc.maricopa.edu/~lsche/proceedings/967_proc/967proc_arendale.htm.

Arendale, D. (2004). Pathways to persistence: A review of postsecondary peer cooperative learning programs. In I. M. Duranczyk, J. L. Higbee, & D. B. Lundell (Eds.). *Best practices for access and retention in higher education* (pp. 27–40). Minneapolis, MN: Center for Research on Developmental Education and Urban Literacy, General College, University of Minnesota.

Lipsky, S. A. (2008). *College study: The essential ingredients*, 2nd ed. Upper Saddle River, NJ: Pearson Prentice Hall Publishers.

Vygotsky, L. S. (1978). *Mind in society: The development of higher psychological processes*. Cambridge, MA: Harvard University Press.

CHAPTER 7

Valuing Diversity among Students

OPENING: LISTENING AND NOTE TAKING

In your sessions, emphasize the importance of taking in-class notes, either written or on a computer. If done well, note taking helps students listen attentively, both in class and in your academic support sessions. Figure 7.1 is a checklist of recommended note taking strategies. Use the checklist to assess your note taking skills; then, use it when you introduce and demonstrate note taking skills with your students.

The problem is not differences among people, but our attitudes regarding these differences.

— Anonymous

FIGURE 7.1 Note taking strategies

	Strategies	Often	Sometimes	Rarely or never	Need more information
Before Class	Skim notes from the previous class				
	Preview corresponding reading assignments				
	Obtain online notes				
	Get supplies (notebook, laptop, pens, books)				

Go to Class!					
During Class	Sit where you readily can see and hear				
	Listen selectively; focus on ideas, not words				
	Write/type the ideas; use phrases & abbrev.				
	Add information to online notes				
	Ask questions; participate in class				
	Leave plenty of open spaces in your notes to add information later				
After Class	Go back over notes soon after class				
	Organize and clarify notes				
	Add related information from text				
	Create potential test questions				
	Review weekly				
	Recite aloud				

ACTIVITY 7.1

NOTE TAKING STRATEGIES

Refer to Figure 7.1.

1. Indicate how often you implement the recommended note taking strategies. If you are unclear about the strategy and need more explanation, place a check in the last column.

2. View the results of the checklist, reflecting on how you might improve your note taking. Choose one strategy that you want to implement for a targeted course. Develop and apply a personal goal regarding your use of the strategy. Adhere to the goal-setting criteria described in Chapter 1:

    ___Be specific.

    ___Be realistic.

Continued

ACTIVITY 7.1 *Continued*

___Have a time constraint.

___Write it down.

___Say it out loud.

___Afterward, evaluate your success.

___Share with another person.

Complete your goal statement. *I will:*

3. After implementing your goal, assess its effectiveness. Consider whether you will continue to use your chosen strategy. Also, think about other methods that you can implement to increase the meaningfulness of your in-class notes.

Thinking About Diversity

INDIVIDUAL ACTIVITY 7.2

REFLECTING

Answer the following three questions. (You will be sharing your answers with classmates.)

A. List three ways in which the student population at your institution is diverse. (Consider areas beyond gender and race.)

B. List two ways that you consider yourself *similar to* others enrolled in the training course.

C. List two ways that you consider yourself *different from* others enrolled in the training course.

GROUP ACTIVITY 7.3

BRAINSTORMING

First, combine everyone's answers for item A. Then, add to the list as you discuss other ways that your student population is diverse. Finally, consider how the diversity of your student population might affect your work as a peer educator.

CREATING A VENN DIAGRAM*

In groups of two to five people, combine answers for items B and C in Activity 7.2. Collaborate to develop a Venn diagram that summarizes similarities and differences among group members. Feel free to incorporate color, design, and other distinctive elements within your diagram. Share your completed Venn diagram with the other groups in your training class.

*A Venn diagram consists of a series of two or more circles representing similarities (overlapping portions) and differences (outer portions) for sets of information. Figure 7.2 shows a Venn diagram summarizing textbook reading and lecture note taking strategies.

FIGURE 7.2 Example of Venn diagram

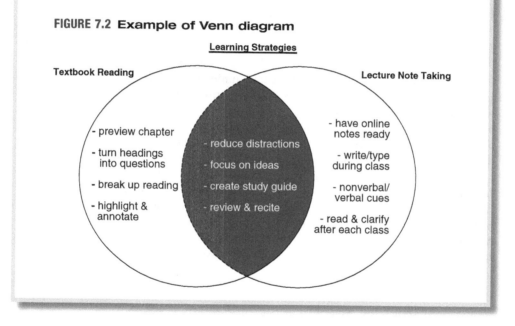

INDIVIDUAL ACTIVITY 7.5

PREDICTING

How do you envision using the previous activities—reflecting, brainstorming, and creating a Venn diagram—in your peer-led sessions? Describe how you might use each learning activity in your work.

Overview

College students today are more diverse than ever. Students reflect the differences within current society, including—but not limited to—variations in race, culture, ethnicity, religion, sexual orientation, ages, and nationality. Students attend college with differing styles, goals, skill levels, values, and experiences. Also, students might have medical limitations or physical or learning disabilities. An awareness of the diversity among students can help you avoid uncomfortable, hurtful, or other detrimental situations in your work. Your goal as a peer educator is to create a comfortable, cohesive setting that allows for productive, collaborative learning. If a potentially hurtful or divisive situation does arise, you need to respond in an appropriate manner so as to maintain your integrity as a leader, as well as the reputation of the overall program for which you work.

Dealing with Differences

Learning is not equal. Students come to college with differing educational backgrounds, cultural perspectives, and family and social experiences, all of which affect how individuals interpret and understand content. Dealing with the array of differences among your peers can be daunting. A practical starting point is to recognize similarities and common ground among students. For example, students probably have mutual goals to achieve high grades in the course or common difficulties with note taking in class. Also, consider the unique characteristics and experiences that each individual brings to the learning process. For example, one student might have gaps in basic math skills but is adept at articulating each step in problem solving. Another student works at a convenience store and provides real-life examples of using math concepts. An older student is very reserved but displays a positive attitude and willingness to work that is contagious among group members. By identifying the uniqueness of students, you learn to appreciate their individuality and become more adept at using individual strengths within your sessions.

ACTIVITY 7.6

IDENTIFYING SIMILARITIES AND DIFFERENCES

- Similar to the chapter's opening activity, consider how students in your academic support sessions are alike. List two similar characteristics.
- How are students in your academic support sessions unique? Identify two students. Write a characteristic that distinguishes each one in a learning setting.

GUIDELINES FOR PEER LEADERS

In your peer leadership role, be prepared to proactively welcome and involve students of differing races, cultures, genders, ages, and backgrounds to your sessions. The following are elements that address common questions about how peer educators can deal appropriately with a diverse student population. You will refer to these elements when observing the role-playing scenarios for Activity 7.8.

How do you create a friendly, open, accepting atmosphere?

___1. Smile. Say hello to each student by name.

___2. Personally invite individual students to attend a session.

___3. Compliment and encourage students. Your kind words show that you recognize and value students, which helps to develop a comfortable and inviting learning environment.

___4. Sit next to a student who seems different in one way or another.

How can you involve each student in sessions?

___5. Incorporate a variety of learning activities that accommodate various learning preferences, styles, and personalities.

___6. Sit next to and encourage students who seem uninvolved.

___7. Talk to a nonparticipating student one-on-one, away from others. Ask the student why he or she is not participating. The student might be feeling insecure about abilities, alienated from the group, intimidated by others who dominate the conversation, or simply unprepared for the sessions.

How should you provide constructive feedback to students without being mean or hurting feelings?

___8. Provide praise for correct answers and for noteworthy efforts. However, do not praise blindly. Praise becomes meaningless and even patronizing when provided too often.

___9. Respond to students' errors. Suggest how students might approach the problem differently or change an answer, as opposed to simply declaring that the students are wrong. Avoid abrupt words or harsh tones that might lead students to think that you are questioning their capabilities.

How can I encourage discussion and participation without creating out-of-control talking and personal attacks?

___10. Set ground rules for group discussion at the beginning of the semester. Prepare students to be exposed to different perspectives and styles of communicating. Insist on respectful reactions to others' points of view.

___11. Don't allow personal criticisms and pointed attacks toward other students or instructors.

___12. Plan ahead of time. Set up activities. Announce time limits.

___13. If discussions do arise that invoke emotions and personal feelings, keep the atmosphere respectful.

___14. Light-hearted humor goes a long way toward diffusing tenseness that arises in a group discussion.

How can I get everyone to participate and to work equally?

___15. From the start, let students know your expectations that each comes prepared to work during the session.

___16. Assign roles for small-group activities. Mix up groups so students are working with new people.

How do you know if students are feeling alienated or excluded in your sessions?

___17. Ask for students' feedback, and then respond to it. Use informal assessment techniques, as described in Chapter 4

___18. If you notice a student is quiet and has not participated, talk to the student privately. Ask about the student's perspective and experiences in the sessions.

What should you do if you hear a prejudiced remark, sexist comment, racial joke, or see an offensive gesture?

___19. Do respond promptly. Clearly state your disapproval, using an even, firm tone of voice. Then, move on to the work at hand.

___20. Don't ignore the comment. Don't pretend that you didn't hear the comment or that the comment is unimportant. Students might interpret your non-reaction as implicit approval on your part. Furthermore, students might think that you are giving them the go-ahead to continue such behaviors.

___21. Set ground rules, and be consistent from the start of the semester.

What should you do if a student repeats a prejudiced remark, sexist comment, racial joke, or offensive gesture?

___22. Ask repeat offenders to leave a session.

___23. Ask your supervisor or other staff member to intervene if a student is disruptive and doesn't follow your directives, in any way bullies others, or distracts from the collective learning.

ACTIVITY 7.7

CASE STUDIES

In each of the case studies, indicate what the peer educator should have done differently. Discuss with others in your training class.

I. At the beginning of a group study/review session, one of the students complains about a course assignment: "I can't believe we have to do all of these questions. This assignment is so gay." The peer educator laughs slightly and says: "I understand your frustration, but you still need to complete the assignment." Another student in the group, Michael, happens to be homosexual. Michael sits quietly and uncomfortably throughout this exchange. After the end of this session, Michael does not return again. *How should the peer educator have handled this scenario differently?*

II. The tutor is working with two students, Ashley and Shane, on a problem. In the course of conversation, Shane makes a vulgar remark about the female course professor. The tutor ignores this remark and moves to assist another student waiting for help. Ashley objects to Shane's language. Shane replies that she should "get a life." This argument escalates, their voices getting louder and louder. *How should the tutor have handled this scenario differently?*

III. In a review session, Shaun hears Nikki make a joke about Muslims being terrorists. Shaun objects to this negative stereotype. Nikki replies: "I was just telling a joke. Where's your sense of humor?" The peer educator says: "I do think that Nikki was just joking." Feeling outnumbered, Shaun leaves the room. The next day in class, he tells other students that the tutorial sessions are a waste of time. *How should the peer educator have handled this scenario differently?*

Resources for Referral

Where do you refer students who have particular problems or concerns that are beyond your role as a peer educator? Figure 7.3 contains a list of common issues that arise with college students. Following each are appropriate on-campus offices or programs, as well as a few off-campus agencies that you can direct students to use. Create a reference guide by filling in contact information about each program—location, phone, website, and so on. If you find other useful programs on your campus or within the surrounding community, add them to the list. Keep this sheet handy to refer to in your work with students.

FIGURE 7.3 Student referral list

1. *You notice a student is struggling because of a language barrier.*
    International Student Office or English as Second Language (ESL) Program

2. *You notice a student has problems writing an essay, including many grammatical errors.*
    Writing Center

3. *A student has failed a number of courses.*
    Advising Center
    Academic Support or Learning Center

4. *A student is unsure about a major.*
    Career Services Office
    Advising Center

5. *You suspect a student might have a learning disability.*
    Office of Student Disability Support Services

6. *A student needs adaptations for a physical disability, such as enlarged print because of poor eyesight or accessible classrooms because of a wheelchair.*
    Office of Student Disability Support Services

Continued

FIGURE 7.3 *Continued*

7. *A student is experiencing technology-related problems.*

    Office of Student Technology Services

8. *A student is a member of an ethnic or religious minority and confides that he or she is feeling isolated.*

    Multicultural Center, African American Cultural Center, Latino Student Center

    Campus Ministry, Hillel Association, or similar religious resource

9. *A student wants to participate in an internship or cooperative education arrangement.*

    Office of Cooperative Education or Internships

10. *A student seems to be anorexic, bulimic, depressed, very anxious, abused, or otherwise troubled. A student is misusing alcohol or drugs.*

    Counseling Center

    Health Center

    Off-campus Counseling Services

    Alcoholics Anonymous or other support group

ACTIVITY 7.8

ROLE-PLAYING SCENARIOS

With others in your class, practice how to respond to each scenario. Have one person act as the peer educator, another act as the student, and the remaining people are observers. Observers use the "Guidelines for Peer Leaders" (p. 89) and the student referral list (Figure 7.3) to critique and provide feedback for the role-playing scenarios.

1. You lead weekly biology study/review sessions for pre-med majors. Six students, five males and one female, attend on a regular basis. You notice that the female, who seems to be attentive, does not volunteer answers or ask questions. You are hesitant to call on her; however, you want her to be involved in the discussion and activities. *How do you handle this situation?*

2. You are a tutor for walk-in homework helper sessions for basic math courses. Many students attend the sessions. On several occasions a student named Chris has asked you a question and you have smelled alcohol on his breath. Today you note that his eyes are bloodshot. *How do you handle this situation?*

3. A nonnative English–speaking student comes quite frequently for tutorial assistance in a variety of social science courses. For the student to understand what you say, you talk slowly and repeat phrases. In addition, you strain to understand the student. Furthermore, you notice that the student is having difficulty reading the textbooks for these courses. *How do you handle this situation?*

4. You have been working with a student in College Chemistry I on a weekly basis for most of the semester. This student is prepared for sessions, having done homework and reviewed notes. In addition, when you review material before a test, the student seems to know the material thoroughly. You are surprised that this student has failed the past two exams. With two more exams left in the semester, the student is very frustrated and discouraged. *How do you handle this situation?*

5. Usually twelve to fifteen students attend your Supplemental Instruction sessions for physics. Three African-American students, who attend regularly, always sit by themselves at a table in the rear of the room. The other students, all of whom are Caucasian, always sit at the other tables. You would like to change this arrangement so that the African-American students are not sitting by themselves. However, you are unsure about what to do. *How do you approach this situation?*

Closing

STEREOTYPES AND BIASES

Practically all people have stereotypes, both positive and negative, that they associate with groups of people. Negative labels and biases are not only hurtful to individuals but detrimental to building community and collaboration among students. As a peer educator, you should be mindful of negative preconceptions and subtle biases that you have about others.

ACTIVITY 7.9

DIFFERENT PERSPECTIVES

Gather a group of coworkers or students in your training class. The ideal size is four to six people in a group. Each person should have a copy of the questions in Figure 7.4.

1. Each person writes his or her answers to the questions listed in Figure 7.4.

2. Then, convene as a group. Each person tells the others his or her answers.

3. As a group, discuss the following: What are examples of stereotypes, prejudices, and favoritism (all of which can be very subtle) that you have encountered in college? As a peer educator, what actions can you take to reduce intolerant attitudes and behaviors that others might display?

Continued

ACTIVITY 7.9 *Continued*

FIGURE 7.4 **Understanding and eliminating stereotypes**

1. Describe yourself in three words.

2. Identify one thing in your background that you value. Think about your family relationships and traditions, ethnic identity, and religious and cultural upbringing.

3. Identify a stereotype that offends you.

4. Describe a situation when you or someone else spoke up or took action following a prejudiced remark. Or identify a time that you *should have* spoken up or taken action regarding a prejudiced remark.

4. This step is personal and private—you are *not* expected to share your answer with others. After the group discussion, identify one personal bias or negative stereotype that you want to eliminate.

5. Refer back to this stereotype or bias periodically throughout the year. Reflect on how successful you have been to eliminate, or at least reduce, your bias.

CONCLUSION

In your peer leadership role, strive to understand, appreciate, and welcome a diverse group. Your academic support sessions should reflect an atmosphere of mutual respect in a comfortable, inclusive, work-oriented setting. By showing students that you value their uniqueness, you will help them to feel at ease attending and participating in your sessions.

Suggestions from Experienced Peer Educators

HOW DO YOU CREATE A WELCOMING SETTING?

I know how important it is to use names, so I developed a way that helps me remember students' names. Students tell me an adjective that: 1) reminds them of themselves and 2) begins with the first letter of their name. For example: "Jell-O John." (Nicole M.)

 Be conscious of displaying a positive, upbeat, and patient attitude toward *each* student. Remember what it was like when you were learning something new and difficult. (Jorge H.)

CHAPTER 8

Online Assistance

Discipline-specific terminology is a vital component of college courses, even entry-level courses. To earn satisfactory course grades, students must go beyond simple memorization of definitions. Students should know how to use and apply terms appropriately in the context of the subject matter. As a peer educator, be prepared to work with students on strategies for learning terms that are totally unfamiliar, as well as terms they might recognize but cannot use independently.

Web-based media can be a tool for learning, a tool for critical thought, and a tool for creating new information.

— Michael Wesch, researcher

of effects of social media

Procedure for Learning Terminology

The following steps assist students to learn vocabulary and jargon associated with a subject.

1. Recognize the discipline-related context of the term. For example, in the context of online assistance, the word "hybrid" refers to a type of course or tutorial program, not a type of car.

2. Know the proper pronunciation of the term. Be able to recognize the word or phrase in speech, as well as in print. Will you be able to identify the term if your instructor uses it in class?

3. Practice using the term in speech and in writing. Apply the term in conversation. Create study cards that include variations of the word, as well as examples and applications. Imitate how you might use the term in class or in a real-life situation. Rehearse applications of the term for a test.

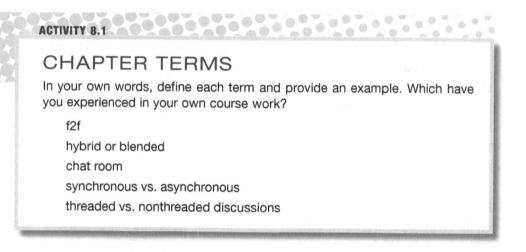

ACTIVITY 8.1

CHAPTER TERMS

In your own words, define each term and provide an example. Which have you experienced in your own course work?

f2f

hybrid or blended

chat room

synchronous vs. asynchronous

threaded vs. nonthreaded discussions

Adjustments for Online Assistance

Whether in an online or traditional setting, the peer educator's role remains the same—to assist students with what to learn, how to learn it, and how to understand it. Likewise, whether face to face or online, the most successful academic support sessions share common components, such as focusing on one chunk of information at a time, activities that include examples and applications of content, adequate time-on-task for students to practice and reflect, and regular feedback. Then again, other components do entail adaptations for online peer-led sessions. The following are recommendations for how peer educators can provide high-quality peer assistance within the steadily growing online venues.

PREPARATION

Before beginning to work with students, it is crucial that you are proficient with the technological system and tools in your institution. If you are working with a specific online course, make sure that you have access to the course. Usually the course instructor grants permission, with the assistance of campus technology services. Course-based peer educators need to be competent navigating the learning-management system (such as Blackboard, Moodle, or WebCT), as well as course components. Become familiar with the syllabus. Learn about course materials—required texts, course units and accompanying assignments, how students will be tested and graded, predicted pace of topics, and other instructor expectations and policies. Finally, know what communication tools you are expected to use in your peer educator role—email, chat sessions, discussion forums, whiteboard, calendar functions, text messaging, wiki activities, and/or other collaboration tools.

Furthermore, practice simulating online interactions and types of situations. Understand program protocols, including how to handle system breakdowns. You want to feel proficient and confident with the technology *before* working with the students.

At the start of the term, you likely will face a range of technology-related questions from students. Do not assume that students with whom you work are proficient with computers and navigating an online delivery system. Some students will have spent a multitude of hours online by the time you interact with them; others will have had minimal technological experience and might be unfamiliar even with basic emailing skills. Because persistent frustrations with technology will turn off students from the start, even before they tackle course content, think in advance about procedures for handling students' questions.

One recommendation is to create clear instructions beforehand regarding how to access and use the technology. This ready-made information should help orient students to the online system and, as a result, reduce greatly the confusion that so often accompanies the start of a semester. Include items such as:

- Institutional default programs for word processing, learning-management systems, web browsing, email, and media files.

- Campuswide network system—what resources are available (drives to access and back up information, printers, PCs, personal web space, wireless network) and how to access these resources.

ACTIVITY 8.2

SUMMARIZE AND APPLY

Figure 8.1 shows the beginnings of a graphic organizer summarizing information in Chapter 8. This chart provides a tool for 1) reviewing and summarizing important ideas in this chapter and 2) thinking about practices for your peer educator position. As you read the chapter, you will stop periodically to fill in more information in the chart. When completed, you will have a study guide to use on the job.

Begin working to complete this graphic organizer: The previous section contained the challenges listed for the topic "Preparation." The corresponding methods for tackling each challenge (found in the last column of Figure 8.1) originated from information presented in this chapter or, as in the case of "Hold a special session...," ideas from readers. Add another method for dealing with each of these two challenges.

Continued

ACTIVITY 8.2 *Continued*

FIGURE 8.1 Challenges of online assistance

Topics	Challenges with online assistance	Ways peer educators can deal with challenges
1. **Preparation**	Peer educator unfamiliar with online system	Before working with students, familiarize yourself with the online system and course components. Practice simulated interactions.
	Students unfamiliar with technology	Create instructions and FAQ beforehand. Hold a special session at the beginning of the semester for students who need help with basic technology.
2. **Asynchronous**	Delayed communication	
	Add another challenge:	
3. **Written Communication**	Monitoring messages	
	Students' inadequate writing skills	Collaborate with the campus writing center to hold workshops and special tutorial sessions.
	Add another challenge:	
4. **Questioning**	Need to guide students toward answers	Let students know in advance that you will not give them answers directly.
	Students' inadequate responses	Provide students with models of thoughtful, reasoned, evidence-based answers.
	Add another challenge:	
5. **Learning Strategies**	Students' weak time management skills	
	Students' procrastination with online work	
	Students' motivation with online course work	Tell students to focus on what they can *learn* in the course, not on the expectation of how easy the course will be.
	Students' poor reading skills	Provide models of how to highlight and annotate online text passages.
	Add another challenge:	
6. **Community**	Students feeling remote and anonymous	Use a "profiles" area.

- Specific directions and information regarding use of campus email. Include how to attach and open documents, as well as the protocol for emailing instructors, administrators, and offices on campus.

- Information cautioning students to check the veracity of online information. Include reputable sites, such as FactCheck.org, for checking authenticity of information. Furthermore, include what constitutes plagiarism, your institution's policies regarding plagiarism, as well as guidelines for citing web materials.

- Campus facilities, such as public computer labs, multimedia areas, and services to train students on how to use technology.

- A section with frequently asked questions (FAQ) and accompanying answers.

- Contact information for student technology services in case students encounter technology-related problems.

In summary, be thoroughly comfortable with the system and protocols before starting your work with students. Adequate preparation will reduce frustrations for you and for the students.

SYNCHRONOUS VERSUS ASYNCHRONOUS

Online assistance is either synchronous or asynchronous. For synchronous assistance, the peer educator and students log on to the system and communicate at the same time. The session is similar to face-to-face assistance in that the peer educator and students work together during an identical, preset time period. Communication often occurs via an online whiteboard, instant message, or chat room.

On the other hand, asynchronous assistance is done at differing times and, therefore, cannot follow the usual discussion format for peer-led sessions. Because of a time delay, asynchronous sessions tend to be more limiting, often following a standard question-and-answer format. For example, a student posts questions online, the peer educator answers these questions at a later time, and still later the student reads the peer educator's answers.

Another limitation of asynchronous sessions is the ability of the peer educator to provide frequent and immediate feedback to students. To compensate for the time delay, the peer educator's remarks tend to be fewer but more encompassing. In other words, in an asynchronous setting, you probably will create fewer comments to each student; however, each comment likely will be longer and cover more topics than in traditional settings.

ACTIVITY 8.3

SUMMARIZE AND APPLY (continued)

Currently, most peer assistance is done in an asynchronous environment. What potential challenges do you envision with asynchronous assistance? Add another challenge in Figure 8.1. Then, add one or two methods for tackling each challenge.

COMMUNICATION

Though the future of online assistance increasingly involves audio and video capabilities, the majority of current programs rely on written communication. Consequently, a challenge for peer educators working in an online environment is the need to communicate in a written format without benefit of spoken words and body language to help communicate ideas.

Writing. Critical for online assistance is your ability to write clearly and precisely. Therefore, be careful of what you write and how you write it, especially since you don't have the benefit of voice inflections and facial and body gestures to help clarify your message.

Simply put, think about what you want to communicate before beginning to write. To get your message across clearly and succinctly, be precise with your language and choice of words. Strive to use correct grammar and spelling. Furthermore, consider the range of your audience; expect students to represent a variety of backgrounds, ages, experiences, values, and sensibilities. Avoid use of slang or potentially offensive verbiage that you may be accustomed to using in messages to friends. Before sending your message, take the time to reread and revise, as necessary. (Providing such thoughtful, accurate written communication is a reason that online learning and instruction requires more time than in face-to-face settings.)

Finally, give students guidelines regarding how to communicate with you and with others. You do not want your online sessions to take on the extreme informality of communication that is typical of text messaging and social networking sites.

ACTIVITY 8.4

SUMMARIZE AND APPLY(continued)

The requirement to communicate by writing produces many potential challenges. For example, peer educators need to monitor their own written messages, as well as the students' messages. In addition, students might not be proficient at constructing clear and readable messages. In Figure 8.1, identify another potential challenge to expect when communicating solely in written format. Then, add ways that you can deal with each challenge associated with written communication.

Questioning. You will be asking and eliciting a multitude of questions in your peer leader role. For both synchronous and asynchronous sessions, questioning is an important communication tool. Be cognizant of the types of questions that you ask. As detailed in Chapter 3, focus on questions that trigger higher-level thinking and that guide students to discovering answers.

Furthermore, provide students with practice asking precise questions and providing solid, accurate responses. Guide students away from relying only on personal beliefs and opinions. Instead, work with them to analyze data, think through their messages, and include concrete examples, pertinent evidence, and solid reasons.

ACTIVITY 8.5

SUMMARIZE AND APPLY(continued)

In Figure 8.1, identify another potential challenge when asking and eliciting questions. Follow up with a practical solution to this challenge.

Communication with instructor. Instructors of online courses frequently are more available than those teaching traditional courses. Email the instructor periodically to provide updates about student usage of online assistance and topics covered during sessions.

ACTIVITY 8.6

CRITIQUE AN ONLINE DIALOGUE

The following dialogue is from an asynchronous tutorial session. The tutor was assigned to provide online assistance to students in multiple sections of the survey course Modern Era History, taught by multiple instructors. After reading the sample dialogue, write your appraisal of this session—what did the tutor do well, and what should the tutor have done differently? In your critique, consider what you just read in the previous section on communication, both writing and questioning.

Student posting: *Help! I am having an essay midterm in Dr. Sherman's class on Monday. He said to expect a question about the 1960s protest movements, and I'm totally confused.*

Tutor posting: *Hello. My name is Tai. I am here to assist you. Please reply back to me with your answers to these questions: 1) What protest movements occurred during the 1960s? Look in your class notes and in your textbook for descriptions of three to four movements. Write back to me with the names of movements and a brief description regarding what they were about. 2) Dr. Sherman usually gives a study guide with sample essay questions for midterm and final exams. Do you have one? If so, are there any questions about the 1960s protest movements?*

Student posting: *Here's what I have from my notes: Civil Rights Movement— freedom from restrictions based on race, Women's Rights Movement— freedom from restrictions based on gender, Vietnam War Protest Movement—freedom from senseless war, American Indian Movement— freedom from restrictions based on race. I also have "freedom from the*

Continued

ACTIVITY 8.6 *Continued*

establishment" written down, but I don't know which one it refers to. Also, I found a question on Dr. Sherman's study guide:"Compare and contrast the 1960s protest movements."

Tutor posting: *A great start! A common theme emerges; your brief descriptions all contain the word "freedom." To adequately answer this essay question, you will need to write about commonalities or similarities of the movements, as well as how each movement is different from one another. I suggest that you make a summary chart to help organize your thoughts. Head each of four columns with the name of a movement. The rows should identify areas to compare and contrast. You can start by making the first row about the movements' theme, "freedom from...." Make each successive row about another area, for example: start of movement, leaders involved, key terms, significant outcomes, why important today. This chart should help clarify similarities and distinctions among the movements. Also, organizing your time is very important since the test is on Monday. I suggest that you complete this a.s.a.p. Good luck!*

LEARNING AND STUDY STRATEGIES

For students enrolled in online courses, a challenge is how to manage their time successfully. Frequently, students are not used to the lack of structure and the amount of independence associated with web-based courses. Students who don't possess the self-discipline and motivation needed to organize their study time tend to procrastinate and fall behind with course work.

Another area of difficulty is the unexpectedly large amounts of reading required for online courses. It is not uncommon for students to have insufficient direction and little practice with how to read long, complex passages independently. As a consequence, students quickly feel overwhelmed with the requirements for online courses.

ACTIVITY 8.7

SUMMARIZE AND APPLY(continued)

Expect that students will need assistance with planning their time, reducing procrastination, motivating themselves to follow through with study plans, and creating techniques for reading and studying multiple sources. These challenges are listed beside the topic "Learning Strategies" in Figure 8.1. Beside each challenge, add recommendations for how peer educators can tackle each. Collaborate with others in your class to come up with an array of techniques to use in your sessions.

COMMUNITY

The online environment can create a sense of anonymity and distantness among students. Thus, work to develop a sense of community in your sessions. The following suggestions should help overcome the feelings of disconnect that can form among students.

Use the "profiles" section of the course-management system. Or create a profiles area for your group of student users via an online discussion board or chat room. Ask all students, yourself included, to post information about their academic majors/minors, interests, technological skills (to assist each other), and a study strategy that has been successful for them. By helping one another with technology and sharing useful learning strategies and study tips, students develop a heightened sense of community.

Furthermore, you might be tempted to give students the answers to their questions, especially given the time delay of asynchronous sessions. However, by redirecting questions back to the other students, you set in motion a sense of mutual purpose and reliance among students. Direct the online conversation so that students get accustomed to discussing content and helping one another with problem areas.

ACTIVITY 8.8

SUMMARIZE AND APPLY(continued)

What are added ways to compensate for the sense of remoteness associated with online venues? Beside the "Community" topic in Figure 8.1, add another suggestion for peer educators.

Closing

ASSESSMENT

For online sessions, incorporate frequent assessment of student learning, just as you do in traditional peer-led sessions. Include opportunities for students to demonstrate that they understand and remember information about each topic. As described in Chapter 4, measuring knowledge of a topic can be quick and informal; the key is to obtain meaningful and concrete evidence of students' understanding.

ACTIVITY 8.9

SUMMATIVE ASSESSMENT

The following questions exemplify a meaningful yet relatively simple way to check your grasp of chapter content. The first two questions are adapted from Cross and Angelo's "One-Minute Paper" (1988).

1. In two to three sentences, summarize the most useful information you learned in this chapter.

2. What is a question you have about online assistance? Or what topic do you want to know more about?

3. Develop a written plan about how you might include online technology in your work with students. Consider using social networking websites (Facebook, MySpace, Twitter), virtual worlds (Second Life), collaborative web pages (wiki), video sharing websites (YouTube), and/or blogs to *enhance learning* for students working on content in your subject area. Ask other peer educators for their feedback regarding your plan.

References

Bromenshenkel, L. (2005, July). *Module 3: Online courses.* PowerPoint presentation for online conference, sponsored by Association for the Tutoring Profession.

Caverly, D. C., & MacDonald, L. (2002). Techtalk: Online learning communities. *Journal of Developmental Education. 25*(3), 36–37.

Cooper, G., Bui, K., & Riker, L. (2000). Protocols and process in online tutoring. (pp. 91–101). In B. Rafoth (Ed.) *A Tutor's Guide, Helping Writers One to One.* Portsmouth, NH: Boynton-Cook Publishers.

Cross, K. P., & Angelo, T. A. (1988). *Classroom assessment techniques: A handbook for faculty.* Ann Arbor, MI: National Center for Research on the Improvement of Postsecondary Teaching and Learning.

Dewey, E. (2005, July). *Training tutors online.* PowerPoint presentation for online conference, sponsored by Association for the Tutoring Profession.

Turrentine, P., & MacDonald, L. (2006, Fall). Tutoring online: Increasing effectiveness with best practices. *NADE Digest. 2*(2), 9–18.

Valenta, A., Therriault, D., Dieter, M., & Mrtek, R. (2001, September). Identifying student attitudes and learning styles in distance education. *Journal of Asynchronous Learning Network, 5*(2), 111–127.

CHAPTER 9

Effective Peer-Led Sessions

A Summary

SUMMATION

An overriding theme throughout this text is elements of effective peer-led sessions, whether one-on-one tutorial or course-based group sessions. As you begin your peer educator position, consider whether you are able to recognize and apply these elements in your own sessions.

Leaders aren't born; they are made. And they are made just like anything else, through hard work. And that's the price we'll have to pay to achieve that goal, or any goal.

— Vince Lombardi, football coach

TOP-TEN LIST

As a means of summarizing content from the previous chapters, create a list of ten core elements that comprise successful peer-led sessions. Scan the preceding chapters as you build your top-ten list. There are no explicitly right or wrong answers for this activity; however, you should be able to justify your answers. Work either by yourself or with others in a small group.

Next, prioritize your ten elements, from most important (#1) to least important (#10). Be prepared to defend your decisions, especially for your top three components.

Finally, each person or group explains his or her list to others in the class. Look for similarities and differences, particularly among the top three items. As a class, can you devise one collaborative top-ten list?

REVISITING YOUR ROLE IN STUDENTS' DEVELOPMENT

The first chapter of this text covered ways that you, the peer educator, might affect the intellectual, psychological, social, and personal development of college students in your academic support sessions. Refer back to Figure 1.2, "Student development and peer educators" (pp. 5–6). For each vector, add one more example of how you can have an impact on students. Share your examples with other peer educators. Keep in mind that topics can overlap and examples can be appropriate for more than one vector.

Self-Assessment

Reflect about your personal strengths and weaknesses as a peer educator. Take into account the top-ten lists created for Activity 9.1. Which elements do you feel comfortable and confident about? Likewise, which elements do you have little experience or practice with?

ACTIVITY 9.3

SELF-ASSESSMENT

1. Identify personal strengths. Describe two to three elements that you feel confident about implementing in your peer educator role. Provide evidence to back up your assessment, such as comments from your supervisor or peer colleagues, content from an observation of your session, a grade on an assignment in your training class, and feedback from students you worked with.

2. Identify something that you want to improve on or try out. For example, if you haven't begun your work as a peer educator, consider doing additional observations of other peer educators' sessions, role-playing and simulations, readings, or discussions with other peer educators. If you have begun working, consider how you might change an undesirable situation (such as a student who misses tutorial appointments or a student who dominates group sessions) or which technique you want to apply (such as pairing students for tutorial appointments or playing a game as review before a test). Or consider trying out one of the suggestions from experienced peer educators located at the end of previous chapters.

Develop and apply a personal goal detailing your plan. Use the criteria described in Chapter 1:

___Be specific.
___Be realistic.
___Have a time constraint.
___Write it down.
___Say it out loud.
___Afterward, evaluate your success.
___Share with another person.

Now, complete your goal statement. *I will:*_____

At the end of your designated time frame, assess the success of your goal statement. Do you need more practice or time, or should you work on another component that would strengthen your preparedness to work as a peer educator? If you tried out a particular technique, analyze its effectiveness. Will you use the strategy again? Should you try something else?

Keep in mind that even experienced peer educators can learn more about ways to approach their role. Thus, periodically assess your work, reflecting on how you might improve.

Conclusion

Vince Lombardi's quote at the beginning of this chapter may be somewhat misleading. Though your development into a strong, effective peer leader does require hard work, this work should be both challenging and rewarding to you. As discussed in Chapter 1, you will gain skills and experiences that should serve you well, not only in your peer educator role, but also in a multitude of future endeavors.

Suggestions from Experienced Peer Educators

WHAT CAN YOU DO WITH AN EMPTY BOX?

Peer educators were asked for ideas about how to use an empty, brightly colored box in their sessions. Here are their creative, yet practical, suggestions:

Students write questions about the course and deposit the questions in the box. These questions are tackled collaboratively during the session. (Theo A.)

Students develop BINGO questions, which are placed in the box. The peer educator draws a question and then calls a letter and number. Before placing a chip on the designated space on their cards, students must correctly answer the question. (Noah W.)

Play the game hot potato. Pass the box around the circle of students. When the music stops, the person holding the box picks a question inside the box. If the student answers it correctly, he or she can stay in the game; otherwise, the person leaves the circle. The last person in the circle wins. (Sadie S.)

The peer educator places a variety of chemistry or math problems in the box. Each student picks a problem to be worked out on the board. (Gavin W.)

At the conclusion of each session, students write practice questions on index cards. This box becomes a test question bank for use in the session before a major test. (Norah A.)

Play the game charades. Write a term, name, or concept on each card. Students pick a card from the box and take turns acting out what is written. The other students guess the correct term. For example, names of sports or professions could be on the cards for Spanish tutoring. Names of personality disorders could be on cards for psychology sessions. (Eva L.)

Play a matching game by putting terms and definitions or equations and problems on cards in the box. (Avinash P.)

Use it as a suggestion box. Students can write anonymous comments about the sessions. (Shiloh B.)

 You add other ideas:_____

INDEX